GW00630504

Irish Lore and Legends

Irish Lore and Legends

Selected and Edited by
S. M. W. Dunnit

THE MERCIER PRESS

The material in this book is based on stories from *Celtic Myths and Legends* by T. W. Rolleston, *The Irish Fairy Book* by A. P. Graves, *Irish Folk and Fairy Legends* by W. B. Yeats, and *Fairy Legends and Traditions of the South of Ireland* by Thomas Crofton Croker.

The illustrations by Susan Sternau interpret previously published drawings from Thomas Crofton Croker's *Fairy Legends and Traditions of the South of Ireland* (1828)—the original illustrator was not credited in that edition.

Mercier Press
PO Box 5, 5 French Church Street, Cork
and 24 Lower Abbey Street, Dublin 1

ISBN 1 85635 078 9

Book design by Charles Ziga, Ziga Design

Printed and bound in the United States of America

MP 9 8 7 6 5 4 3 2 1

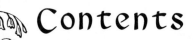

Contents

A Legend of Knockmany

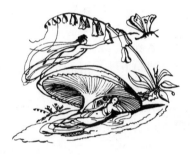

It once happened that a giant named Finn and his gigantic relatives were all working at the Giant's Causeway in order to make a bridge, or what was still better, a good stout pad-road across to Scotland, when Finn, who was very fond of his wife, Oonagh, took it into his head that he would go home and see how the poor woman got on in his absence. So he pulled up a fir tree, and after lopping off the roots and branches, made a walking stick of it and set out on his way to Oonagh.

Finn lived at this time on Knockmany Hill, which faces Cullamore, that rises up, half hill, half mountain, on the opposite side.

The truth is that honest Finn's affection for his wife was

by no means the whole cause of his journey home. There was at that time another giant, named Far Rua—some say he was Irish and some say he was Scottish—but whether Scotch or Irish he was a *targer*. No other giant of the day could stand before him; and such was his strength that, when well vexed, he could give a stamp that shook the country about him.

The face and name of him went far and near, and nothing in the shape of a man, it was said, had any chance with him in a fight. The report went that by one blow of his fist he flattened a thunderbolt, and kept it in his pocket in the shape of a pancake to show to all his enemies when they were about to fight him. Undoubtedly he had given every giant in Ireland a considerable beating, barring Finn M'Coul himself, and he swore that he would never rest night or day, winter or summer, until he could serve Finn with the same sauce, if he could catch him. Finn, however, had a strong disinclination to meet a giant who could make a young earthquake or flatten a thunderbolt when he was angry. So accordingly he kept dodging about from place to place—not much to his credit as a Trojan, to be sure—whenever he happened to get the hard word that Far Rua was on the scent of him. And the long and short of it was that he heard Far Rua was coming to the Causeway to have a trial of strength with him. Finn was seized in consequence with a very warm and sudden fit of affection for his wife, who was delicate in her health, and leading, besides, a very lonely, uncomfortable life of it in his absence.

"God save all her," said Finn good-naturedly, putting his honest face into his own door.

"*Musha*, Finn, *avick*, an' you're welcome to your own

Oonagh, you darlin' bully." Here followed a smack that is said to have made the waters of the lake curl, as it were, with kindness and sympathy.

"Faith," said Finn, "beautiful, and how are you, Oonagh—and how did you sport your figure during my absence, my bilberry?"

"Never a merrier—as bouncing a grass widow as ever there was in sweet 'Tyrone among the bushes.'"

Finn gave a short, good-humored cough, and laughed most heartily to show her how much he was delighted that she made herself happy in his absence.

"An' what brought you home so soon, Finn?" said she.

"Why, *avourneen*," said Finn, putting in his answer in the proper way, "never the thing but the purest of love and affection for yourself. Sure, you know that's the truth, anyhow, Oonagh."

Finn spent two or three happy days with Oonagh, and felt himself very comfortable considering the dread he had of Far Rua. This, however, grew upon him so much that his wife could not but perceive something lay on his mind which he kept altogether to himself.

"It's this Far Rua," said he upon her questioning, "that's troublin' me. When the fellow gets angry and begins to stamp he'll shake you a whole townland, and it's well known that he can stop a thunderbolt, for he always carries one with him in the shape of a pancake to show to anyone that might misdoubt it."

As he spoke he clapped his thumb in his mouth, as he always did when he wanted to prophesy or to know anything.

"He's coming," said Finn, "I see him below at Dungannon."

"An' who is it, *avick?*"

"Far Rua," replied Finn, "and how to manage I don't know. If I run away I am disgraced, and I know that sooner or later I must meet him, for my thumb tells me so."

"When will he be here?" she asked.

"Tomorrow, about two o'clock," replied Finn with a groan.

"Don't be cast down," said Oonagh, "depend on me, and, maybe, I'll bring you out of this scrape better than ever you could bring yourself."

This quieted Finn's heart very much, for he knew that Oonagh was hand-and-glove with the fairies; and indeed, to the truth, she was supposed to be a fairy herself. If she was, however, she must have been a kind-hearted one, for by all accounts she never did anything but good in the neighborhood.

Now, it so happened that Oonagh had a sister named Granua living opposite to them, on the very top of Cullamore and this Granua was quite as powerful as herself. The beautiful valley that lies between the Granlisses is not more than three or four miles broad, so that of a summer evening Granua and Oonagh were able to hold many an agreeable conversation across it, from one hilltop to the other. Upon this occasion Oonagh resolved to consult her sister as to what was best to be done in the difficulty that surrounded them.

"Granua," said she, "are you at home?"

"No," said the other, "I'm picking blueberries at Althadhawan."

"Well," said Oonagh, "go up to the top of Cullamore, look about you, and then tell us what you see."

"Very well," replied Granua, after a few minutes, "I am there now."

"What do you see?" asked the other.

"Goodness be about us!" exclaimed Granua, "I see the biggest giant that ever was known coming up from Dungannon."

"Aye," said Oonagh, "there's our difficulty. That's Far Rua, and he's comin' up now to leather Finn. What's to be done?"

"I'll call to him," she replied, "to come up to Cullamore and refresh himself, and maybe that will give you and Finn time to think of some plan to get yourselves out of the scrape. But," she proceeded, "I'm short of butter, having in the house only half a dozen *firkins*, and as I'm to have a few giants and giantesses to spend the evenin' with me I'd feel thankful, Oonagh, if you'd throw me up fifteen or sixteen tubs, or the largest *miscaun* you've got, and you'll oblige me very much."

"I'll do that with a heart and a half," replied Oonagh, "and, indeed, Granua, I feel myself under great obligations to you for your kindness in keeping him off us until we see what can be done, for what would become of us if anything happened to Finn, poor man?"

She accordingly got the *miscaun* of butter she had—which might be about the weight of a couple of dozen millstones—and calling up to her sister, "Granua," said she, "are you ready? I'm going to throw you up a *miscaun*, so be prepared to catch it."

"I will," said the other. "A good throw, now, and take care it does not fall short."

Oonagh threw it, but in consequence of her anxiety about Finn and Far Rua she forgot to say the charm that was to send it up, so that instead of reaching Cullamore, as she expected, it fell about half way between the two hills at the edge of the Broad Bog, near Augher.

"Never mind," said Granua, "I must only do the best I can with Far Rua. If all else fails, I'll give him a cast of heather broth, or a paste of oak bark. But, above all things, think of some plan to get Finn out of the scrape he's in, or he's a lost man. You know you used to be sharp and ready-witted; and my opinion is, Oonagh, that it will go hard with you, or you'll outdo Far Rua yet."

She then made a high smoke on the top of the hill, after which she put her finger in her mouth and gave three whistles, and by that Far Rua knew that he was invited to the top of Cullamore—for this was a sign to all strangers and travelers to let them know they were welcome to come and take share of whatever was going on.

In the meantime Finn was very melancholy, and did not know what to do, or how to act at all. Far Rua was an ugly customer, and moreover the idea of the confounded "cake" aforesaid flattened the very heart within him. What chance could he have, strong and brave as he was, with a man who could, when put in a passion, walk the country into earthquakes and knock thunderbolts into pancakes? The thing was impossible, and Finn knew not on what hand to turn him. Right or left, backward or forward, where to go he could form no guess whatever.

"Oonagh," said he, "can you do anything for me? Where's all your creativity? Am I to be skivered like a rabbit before your eyes and to have my name disgraced forever in the sight of all my tribe, and me the best man among them? How am I to fight this man-mountain—this huge cross

between an earthquake and a thunderbolt—with a pancake in his pocket that was once—?"

"Be aisy, Finn," replied Oonagh. "Troth, I'm ashamed
of you. Keep your toe in your pump, will you? Talking of
pancakes, maybe we'll give him as good as any he brings
with him—thunderbolts or otherwise. If I don't treat him
to as smart a feeding as he's got this many a day, don't
trust Oonagh again. Leave him to me, and do just as I
bid you."

This relieved Finn very much, for, after all, he had great
confidence in his wife, knowing, as he did, that she had
got him out of many a quandary before. The present,
however, was the greatest of all, but still he began to get
courage and to eat his victuals as usual. Oonagh then
drew the nine woolen threads of different colors, which
she always did to find out the best way of succeeding in
anything of importance. She then plaited them into three
plaits, with three colors in each, putting one on her right
arm, one around her heart, and the third around her right
ankle, for then she knew that nothing could fail her that
she undertook.

Having everything now prepared, she went around to
the neighbors and borrowed twenty-one iron griddles,
which she took and kneaded into the hearts of twenty-
one cakes of bread, and these she baked on the fire in
the usual way, setting them aside in the cupboard as they
were done. She then put down a large pot of new milk,
which she made into curds and whey, and gave Finn due
instructions how to use the curds when Far Rua should
come. Having done all this, she sat down quite contented waiting for his arrival on the next day about two o'clock,
that being the hour at which he was expected—for Finn

knew as much by the sucking of his thumb.

Now this was a curious property that Finn's thumb had; but not withstanding all the wisdom and logic he used to suck out of it, it was no good in this situation without the wit of his wife. In this very thing, moreover, he very much resembled his great foe, Far Rua; for it was well known that the huge strength that he possessed all lay in the middle finger of his right hand, and that if he happened by any chance to lose it, he was no more, notwithstanding his bulk, than a common man.

At length the next day he was seen coming across the valley, and Oonagh knew that it was time to commence operations. She immediately made the cradle and desired Finn to lie down in it and cover himself up.

"You must pass for your own child," said she, "so just lie there snug and say nothing, but be guided by me."

This, to be sure, seemed very cowardly to Finn, but he knew Oonagh very well and finding that he had nothing else for it, with a very rueful face he gathered himself into it and lay snug, as she had desired him.

About two o'clock, as he had expected, Far Rua came in. "God save all here!" said he. "Is this where the great Finn M'Coul lives?"

"Indeed it is, honest man," replied Oonagh. "God save you kindly—won't you be sitting?"

"Thank you, ma'am," he said, sitting down. "You're Mrs. M'Coul, I suppose?"

"I am," said she, "and I have no reason, I hope, to be ashamed of my husband."

"No," said the other, "he has the name of being the strongest and bravest man in Ireland. But, for all that, there's a man not far from you that's very anxious of taking a shake with him. Is he at home?"

"Why, no, then," she replied, "and if ever a man left in a fury he did. It appears that someone told him of a big *bosthoon* of a giant called Far Rua being down at the Causeway to look for him, and so he set out there to try if he could catch him. Troth, I hope, for the poor giant's sake, he won't meet with him, for if he does Finn will make paste of him at once."

"Well," said the other, "I am Far Rua, and I have been seeking him these twelve months, but he always kept clear of me. I will never rest day or night until I lay my hands on him."

At this Oonagh set up a loud laugh of great contempt and looked at him as if he were only a mere handful of a man.

"Did you ever see Finn?" said she, changing her manner all at once.

"How could I?" said he. "He always took care to keep his distance."

"I thought so," she replied. "I judged as much. If you take my advice, you poor-looking creature, you'll pray night and day that you may never see him, for I tell you it will be a black day for you when you do. But, in the meantime, you perceive that the wind's on the door, and as Finn himself is far from home, maybe you'd be civil enough to turn the house, for it's always what Finn does when he's here."

This was a startler, even to Far Rua. He got up, however, and after pulling the middle finger of his right hand until it cracked three times, he went outside, and getting his arms about the house, completely turned it as she had wished. When Finn saw this he felt a certain description of moisture, which shall be nameless, oozing out through every pore of his skin, but Oonagh, depending upon her woman's wit, felt not a whit daunted.

"Arrah, then," said she, "as you're so civil, maybe you'd do another obliging turn for us, as Finn's not here to do it himself. You see, after this long stretch of dry weather that we've had, we feel very badly off for want of water. Now, Finn says there's a fine spring well somewhere under the rocks behind the hill there below, and it was his intention to pull them asunder. But after having heard of you he left the place in such a fury that he never thought of it. Now, if you try to find it, troth, I'd feel it kindness."

She then brought Far Rua down to see the place, which was then all one solid rock; and after looking at it for some time, he cracked his right middle finger nine times. Stooping down, he tore a cleft about four hundred feet deep and a quarter of a mile in length, which has since been christened by the name of Lumford's Glen. This feat nearly threw Oonagh herself off guard, but it wasn't enough to throw a woman's sagacity and presence of mind.

"You'll now come in," said she, "and eat a bit of such humble fare as we can give. Finn, even though you and he were enemies, would scorn not to treat you kindly in his own house; and, indeed, if I didn't do it even in his absence, he would not be pleased with me."

She accordingly brought him in, and placing half a dozen of the cakes spoken of earlier before him, together with a can or two of butter, a side of boiled bacon, and a stack of cabbage, she desired him to help himself. Far Rua, who was a glutton as well as a hero, put one of the cakes in his mouth to take a huge whack out of it, when both Finn and Oonagh were stunned with a noise that resembled something between a growl and a yell.

"Blood and fury!" he shouted out. "How is this? Here are two of my teeth out! What kind of bread is this you gave me?"

"What's the matter?" said Oonagh coolly.

"Matter!" shouted the other. "Why, here are two of the best teeth in my head gone."

"Why," said she, "that's Finn's bread—the only bread he ever eats when at home; but, indeed, I forgot to tell you that nobody can eat it but himself and that child in the cradle there. I thought, however, that as you were reported to be rather a stout little fellow of your size you might be able to manage it, and I did not wish to affront a man that thinks himself able to fight Finn. Here's another cake—maybe it's not so hard as that."

Far Rua, at the moment, was not only hungry, but ravenous, so he made another fresh set at the second cake, and immediately another yell was heard twice as loud as the first.

"Thunder and giblets!" he roared, "take your bread out of this, or I will not have a tooth in my head; there's another pair of them gone."

"Well, honest man," replied Oonagh, "if you're not able to eat the bread say so quietly, and don't be awakening the child in the cradle there. There, now, he's awake upon me!"

Finn now gave a *skirl* that frightened the giant, as coming from such a youngster as he was represented to be.

"Mother," said he, "I'm hungry—get me something to eat."

Oonagh went over, and putting into his hand a cake that had no griddle in it—Finn, whose appetite in the meantime was sharpened by what he saw going forward, soon made it disappear. Far Rua was thunderstruck and secretly thanked his stars that he had the good fortune to miss meeting Finn.

"I'd have no chance with a man who could eat such bread as that, which even his son that's in the cradle can munch before my eyes," thought Far Rua.

He then said to Oonagh, "I'd like to take a glimpse at that lad in the cradle for I can tell you that the infant who can manage that nutriment is no joke to look at or to feed of a scarce summer."

"With all the veins of my heart," replied Oonagh. "Get up, *acushla*, and show this decent little man something that won't be unworthy of your father, Finn M'Coul."

Finn, who was dressed for the occasion as much like a boy as possible, got up and asked, "Are you strong?"

"Thunder and ounze!" exclaimed the other, "What a voice in so small a chap!"

"Are you strong?" said Finn again. "Are you able to squeeze water out of that white stone?" he asked, putting one into Far Rua's hand.

The latter squeezed and squeezed the stone, but to no purpose. He might pull the rocks of Lumford's Glen asunder and flatten a thunderbolt, but to squeeze water out of a white stone was beyond his strength. Finn eyed him with great contempt as he kept straining and squeezing and squeezing and straining until he got black in the face with the efforts.

"Ah, you're a poor creature," said Finn. "You a giant! Give me the stone here, and when I show what Finn's little son can do you may then judge of what my daddy himself is."

Finn then took the stone and slyly exchanged it for the curds. He squeezed the latter until the whey, as clear as water, oozed out in a little shower from his hand.

"I'll now go in," said he, "to my cradle, for I scorn to lose my time with anyone that's not able to eat my daddy's bread, or squeeze water out of a stone. You had better be off out of this before he comes back, for if he catches you, it's in flummery he'd have you in two minutes."

Far Rua, seeing what he had seen, was of the same opinion himself, his knees knocked together with terror of Finn's return, and he accordingly hastened in to bid Oonagh farewell, and to assure her that, from that day out, he never wished to hear of, much less to see, her husband.

"I admit fairly that I'm not a match for him," said he, "strong as I am. Tell him I will avoid him as I would the plague and that I will make myself scarce in this part of the country while I live."

Finn, in the meantime, had gone into the cradle, where he lay very quietly, his heart in his mouth with delight that Far Rua was about to take his departure without discovering the tricks that had been played off on him.

"It's well for you," said Oonagh, "that he doesn't happen to be here, for it's nothing but hawk's meat he'd make of you."

"I know that," said Far Rua, "divil a thing else he'd make of me; but, before I go, will you let me feel what kind of teeth they are that can eat griddle-cakes like that?" and he pointed to it as he spoke.

"With all the pleasure in life," said she, "only as they're far back in his head you must put your finger a good way in."

Far Rua was surprised to find so powerful a set of grinders in one so young, but he was still much more so on finding, when he took his hand from Finn's mouth, that he had left the very finger upon which his whole strength depended behind him. He gave one loud groan and fell down at once with terror and weakness. This was all Finn wanted, who now knew that his most powerful and bitterest enemy was completely at his mercy. He instantly started out of the cradle, and in a few minutes the great Far Rua, that was for such a length of time the terror of him and all his followers, was no more. ❡

Diarmid Bawn, the Piper

One stormy night Patrick Burke was seated by the fire, smoking his pipe quite contentedly after a hard day's work. His two little boys were roasting potatoes in the ashes while his lovely daughter held a candle for her mother, who, seated on a stool, was mending Patrick's old coat. Judy, the maid, was singing merrily to the sound of her wheel, which made a beautiful humming noise, just like the sweet drone of a bagpipe. Indeed they all seemed quite contented and happy, for the storm howled without and they were all warm and snug within.

"I was just thinking," Patrick said, taking his long-stemmed pipe from his mouth and giving it a rap with his thumbnail to shake out the ashes. "I was just thinking how thankful we all ought to be to have a snug bit of a cabin over our heads on this dank and dreadful night. For in all my born days, I have never heard the like of it."

"And that's no lie for you, Pat," said Molly, his wife. She smiled at Patrick for a moment and then she jumped in her seat. "Quiet!" she whispered harshly. "What noise is that I heard?" She dropped her sewing upon her knees and looked fearfully towards the door.

"The Virgin defend us!" cried Judy as she rapidly made a pious sign across her forehead. "It's the banshee!"

"Hold your tongue, you fool," said Patrick, "it's only the old gate swinging in the wind!" and he had scarcely spoken when the door was assailed by a violent knocking.

Molly began to mumble her prayers and Judy proceeded to mutter over the roll-call of saints. The youngsters scampered off to hide themselves behind the bed while the storm howled louder and more fiercely than ever. The rapping was renewed with increasing violence.

"Quiet," said Patrick, "what a noise you're all making about nothing at all. Judy, can't you go and see who's at the door?" for, bravado notwithstanding, Pat Burke preferred that the maid should open the door.

"You want me to open the door?" said Judy in a tone of astonishment. "Are you raving mad, Mr. Burke? Or do you want me to be taken away like my grandfather before me, never to return? No, I don't think I will open the door, Mr. Burke, and if you were half the man you claim to be, you would do it yourself."

"Very well then!" So saying, Patrick arose, and made his way, as best he could, toward the door. "Who's there?" Patrick shouted, with more than a hint of tremolo. "In the name of Saint Patrick, who is there?"

"It is I, Pat," answered a voice which Pat immediately knew to be the young squire's. Without hesitating, Patrick opened the door and in walked a young man with a gun in his hand. Outside a pack of hunting dogs stood in the rain.

"Your honor's honor is quite welcome in my humble home," said Patrick, who was a very civil sort of fellow, especially to his betters. "If you would please be so condescending as to demean yourself by taking off your wet jacket, Molly can give you a brand new blanket and you can sit before the fire while your clothes are drying."

"Thank you, Pat," the squire said as he wrapped himself up in the woolen blanket. "I was wondering, though, whatever made you keep me so long at the door?"

"Why then, your honor, it was because of Judy, there, being so much afraid of the Little People. Of course, she has good reason, after what happened to her grandfather—the Lord rest his soul!"

"And what was that Pat?" asked the squire.

"Well, your honor, I'll tell you the story."

Judy's grandfather, old Diarmid Bawn, was a piper by trade and as personable a man as you can find in all five parishes. Diarmid could play those pipes of his so sweetly, and make them speak to such perfection, that it did one's heart good to hear him. No one on this side of the country, before or after, could play like Diarmid Bawn— except maybe James Gandsey, the piper for Lord Headly. Mister Gandsey's music is quite good; but other than James Gandsey, there was never a man who could play pipes like Judy's grandfather. Well, old Diarmid lived on a small farm in the mountains. One night he was walking about the fields, quite melancholy for the want of tobacco. The river was flooded and he couldn't get across to buy any, and Diarmid would rather to go to bed without his supper than go a night without his pipe. So, Diarmid was walking his fields because he could not sleep and just as he came to the old fort in the far field out yonder, what should he see? Lord preserve us! It was a large army of Little People scattered about for all the world to see.

"Are you all ready?" cried a little fellow at their head dressed like a general.

"No," said a wee curmudgeon of a chap all dressed in red, from the crown of his cocked hat to the sole of his boot. "No, general," said the curmudgeon, "if you don't get Lord Fir-Darrig a horse, he must stay behind—for he cannot run across the open sea like us. Without Lord Fir-Darrig, we will surely be defeated by those Jamaican dogs!"

"You have a point," the general said to the curmudgeon. Then he looked up at Diarmid Bawn with a gleam in his eye. He pointed at Judy's grandfather, who was a brave man, but frightened nonetheless. "Make a horse out of him."

With that, Lord Fir-Darrig stepped out from the crowd and came up to Diarmid. Lord Fir-Darrig was a mite of a thing, a little red imp grinning a horrible grin. He was dressed head to toe in tiny ringlets of armor, ready for a fight. Diarmid was shaking to the bottom of his boots but he was determined to put on a brave face. He didn't fancy becoming a horse but there didn't seem to be much he could do to stop it. So, he began to cross himself and say some blessed words that nothing bad could stand against.

"You think that'll make a pebble's difference in the

ocean?" said Lord Fir-Darrig, whose voice sounded like a crying baby's. "I don't care three hairs for your empty words or your useless crossings." Without a moment more for Diarmid to react, the imp rapped him with the flat of his sword. In but a moment's time, Diarmid was changed to a horse with little Fir-Darrig stuck on his back.

With Lord Fir-Darrig mounted up, they all flew over the wide ocean, like wild geese, gibbering and screaming all the while. At last, they came to the shores of far-off Jamaica and there they had a war with the Little People of that land. Both sides engaged, and they were fighting splen-didly, as fiercely as men three times their size, until one of those Jamaican men made a cut with his sword under Diarmid's left eye. Well, old Diarmid had had a bad night, and that made him lose his temper entirely. He dashed right into the middle of the fray, with Lord Fir-Darrig mounted up on his back. He threw out his heels. He kicked and he bit. He threw his tail and he wheeled and turned at such a rate that soon the area around him was clear. At last, Diarmid's faction got the upper hand, all because of him. Soon, the Jamaican Little People were routed and there was such feasting and rejoicing as Diarmid had never seen. All agreed that Diarmid Bawn was the greatest horse to be had and they gave him the best of the spoils.

"Let every man fill his pockets with tobacco for Diarmid Bawn!" shouted the general, and so they did. When the celebration had died out, they flew off homeward, Fir-Darrig still mounted on Diarmid's back. Once they reached the old fort over yonder, they vanished like the mist from the mountains.

When Diarmid looked about, the sun was rising. He

thought it was all a dream until he saw the barrel full of tobacco in the old fort. When he saw that he reached up and felt the blood trickling down from his left eye. Sure enough, he had been wounded in the battle. He got up at once, ready to run back home, when he remembered the heaping pile of tobacco in the old fort. Maybe the night hadn't been so bad after all, he thought. As he walked toward the fort, pulling out his pipe, he heard a voice in the distance like a crying baby.

"It's all yours," the voice cried out, "for your good behavior in the battle. If I ever need a horse again, I know where to find the cleverest and strongest in all of Ireland."

"And ever since that day, your honor, the Bawns have been mighty frightened that the Little People might come and make them horses, or milk cows, or some other such thing that a man never ought to be," said Patrick Burke as he finished his tale.

The squire sat for a time, mulling the story over. "Thank you, Pat," he said, "It was certainly a wonderful story and I am no longer surprised by Judy's alarm. But now, as the storm is over, and the moon is shining brightly, I'll make the best of my way home." With that, the squire cast off the blanket they had given him, put on his coat and, whistling for his dogs, set off across the mountains.

Patrick ran to the door and yelled after him "May God and the blessed Virgin herself preserve you and keep you clear of the Little People, your honor! For, it was on a moonlit night like this, so many years ago, that Diarmid Bawn was made a horse for Lord Fir-Darrig to ride!"

The Hillman and the Housewife

There once lived a certain Housewife who had a sharp eye to her own interests, and gave alms of what she had no use for, but she did this only for the good of her soul. The Good People of the hills on the other hand, are very kind-hearted and generous, but they also do not tolerate being treated poorly.

One day a Hillman knocked at the Housewife's door.

"Can you lend us a saucepan, good mother?" he said. "There's a wedding on the hill and all the pots are in use."

"Is he to have one?" asked the servant lass who had opened the door.

"Aye, to be sure," answered the Housewife. "One must be neighborly."

But when the maid was taking a saucepan from the shelf, the Housewife pinched her arm and whispered sharply "Not that, you slut! Get the old one out of the cupboard. It leaks, and the Hillmen are so neat and such nimble workers that they are sure to mend it before they send it home. So one obliges the Good People and saves a sixpence in tinkering. You'll never learn to be notable while your head is on your shoulders."

Thus reproached, the maid fetched the saucepan, which had been set aside till the tinker's next visit, and gave it to the dwarf who thanked her and went on his way.

In due time the saucepan was returned and, as the Housewife had foreseen, it was neatly mended and ready for use.

At supper time the maid filled the pan with milk and set it on the fire for the children's supper. But in a few minutes the milk smoked and was so burnt that no one could touch it, even the pigs refused their food into which it was thrown.

"Ah, good-for-nothing hussy!" cried the Housewife, as she refilled the pan herself, "you would ruin the richest with your carelessness. There's a whole quart of good milk wasted at once!"

"*And that's twopence,*" cried a voice which seemed to come from the chimney in a whining tone like some nattering, discontented old body with grievances.

The Housewife had not left the saucepan for two minutes, when the milk boiled over smoking and burnt as before.

"The pan must be dirty," muttered the good woman in great vexation "and there are two full quarts of milk as good as thrown to the dogs."

"*And that's fourpence,*" added the voice in the chimney.

After a thorough cleaning the saucepan was once more

filled and set on the fire, but with no better success. The milk was hopelessly spoiled and the Housewife shed tears of vexation at the waste crying, "Never before has such a thing befallen me since I've kept house! Three quarts of new milk burnt for one meal!"

"*And that's sixpence,*" cried the voice from the chimney. "*You didn't save the tinker after all, mother!*"

With which words the Hillman himself came tumbling down the chimney and went off laughing through the door, and from that day forward the saucepan was as good as any other. ❧

The Haunted Wine Cellar

The Mac Carthies were one of the old Irish families, with true Milesian blood running in their veins as thick as buttermilk—there were the Mac Carthy-mores, and the Mac Carthy-reaghs, and the Mac Carthies of Muskerry, and all of them were noted for their hospitality to strangers. But no man going by this or by any other name exceeded Justin Mac Carthy of Ballinacarthy at putting food and drink upon his table, and there was a right hearty welcome for everyone who would share it with him.

Many a wine cellar would be ashamed to bear the name alongside that at Ballinacarthy, for it was so exceptionally large, and crowded with bins of wine, and long rows of pipes, and hogsheads and casks, that it would take more time to count than any sober man could spare in such a place.

There are many, no doubt, who would think that a butler would have little to complain of in such a house, and the whole country would certainly have agreed with them if only a man could be found to remain as Mr. Mac Carthy's butler for any length of time worth speaking of, yet not a one who had been in his service gave him a bad word.

"We have no fault to find with the master," they would say, "and if he could but get any one to fetch his wine from the cellar, we might every one of us have grown gray in the house, and have lived there quiet and contented until the end of our days."

Now young Jack Leary, a lad who had been brought up in the stables at Ballinacarthy and had occasionally himself lent a hand in the butler's pantry, thought this to be a queer thing indeed, and he allowed to himself as how if the master would but make him his butler, there would be no more grumbling at his bidding to go to the wine cellar. Young Leary accordingly watched for what he conceived to be a favorable opportunity of presenting himself to the notice of his master.

A few mornings later, Mr. Mac Carthy went into his stable yard rather earlier than usual, and called loudly for the groom to saddle his horse, as he intended going out with the hounds. But there was no groom to answer, and young Jack Leary led Rainbow out of the stable.

"Where is William?" inquired Mr. Mac Carthy.

"Why to tell the truth, sir, he had just a drop too much last night," replied Jack.

"Where did he get it?" said Mr. Mac Carthy, "for since Thomas went away, the key of the wine cellar has been in my pocket, and I have been obliged to fetch what was drunk by myself."

"Sorrow, that I do not know, unless it was the cook who gave him a taste," said Leary. He bowed low to the ground, then spoke again, saying "Sir, may I make so bold as just to ask your honor one question?"

"Speak out, Jack," said Mr. Mac Carthy.

"Why, then, does your honor want a butler?"

"Can you recommend me one," replied his master, with a smile on his face, "who will not be afraid of going to my wine cellar?"

"Is the wine cellar all the matter?" said young Leary. "Devil a doubt I have of myself then for that."

"So you mean to offer me your services in the capacity of butler?" said Mr. Mac Carthy, with some surprise.

"Exactly so," replied young Leary, now for the first time looking up from the ground.

"Well, I believe you to be a good lad, and have no objection to give you a trial."

"Long may your honor reign over us, and the Lord spare you to us!" cried Leary, with another enormous bow, as his master rode off, and he continued for some time to gaze after him with a vacant stare, which slowly and gradually assumed a look of importance.

"Jack Leary," said he at length, "Jack—is it Jack? Faith, 'tis not Jack now, but Mr. John, the butler," and with an air of importance he strode out of the stable toward the kitchen, kicking his elderly hound Bran out of the way, and forgetting completely about pretty Peggy, the kitchen maid whose heart he had assailed the preceding week by the offer of a gold ring for her hand and a lusty imprint of good will upon her lips.

When Mr. Mac Carthy returned from hunting, he sent for Jack Leary—for so he still continued to call his new butler.

"Jack," said he, "I believe you are a trustworthy lad, and here are the keys of my cellar. I have asked the gentlemen with whom I hunted today to dine with me, and I hope they will be satisfied at the way in which you will wait on them at table, but, above all, let there be no want of wine after dinner."

Now Mr. John the butler, having a tolerably quick eye for such things, and being naturally a handy lad, spread his cloth accordingly, laid his plates and knives and forks in the same manner he had seen his predecessors perform these mysteries, and really, for the first time, got through attendance on dinner very well.

It must not be forgotten, however, that the company of booted and spurred fox hunters dining at the house of this Irish country squire, though all excellent and worthy men in their way, did not much care whether the punch produced after the soup was made of Jamaica or Antigua rum, and some even would not have been inclined to question the correctness of good old Irish whiskey.

It was waxing near midnight, when Mr. Mac Carthy rang the bell three times. This was a signal for more wine, and Jack proceeded to the cellar to procure a fresh supply, but it must be confessed not without some little hesitation.

The luxury of ice was then unknown in the south of Ireland, but the superiority of cool wine had been acknowledged by all men of sound judgment and true taste. Mr. Mac Carthy's grandfather was fully aware of this important fact, and so he had the mansion of Ballinacarthy built upon the site of an old castle which had belonged to his ancestors, and in the construction of his magnificent wine cellar had availed himself of a deep vault, excavated from the solid rock in former times as a place of retreat and security. The descent to this vault was by a flight of steep stone stairs, and here and there in the wall were narrow crevices and projections, which cast deep shadows, and looked very frightful when anyone went down the cellar stairs with a single light. Indeed, two lights did not much improve the matter, for though the breadth of the shadows became less, the narrow crevices remained as dark or darker than ever before.

Summoning up all his newfound courage and resolution, down to the vault went Mr. John the butler, bearing in his right hand a lantern and the key of the cellar, and in his left a basket, which he considered sufficiently capacious to contain an adequate stock for the rest of the evening. He arrived at the door without any interruption whatever, but when he put the key, which was of an ancient and clumsy kind, into the lock and turned it, he thought he heard a strange kind of laughing within the cellar, to which unpleasant sound some empty bottles that stood upon the floor outside vibrated so violently that they struck against each other.

Jack Leary paused for a moment, and looked about him with caution. He then boldly seized the handle of the key, and turned it in the lock with all his strength, as if he doubted his own power of doing so, and the door flew open with a most tremendous crash, so that, if the house had not been built upon solid rock, he would have shook it from the foundations.

To recount what the poor fellow saw would be impossible, for he seems not to know very clearly himself, but what he told the cook the next morning was that he heard a roaring and bellowing like a mad bull, and that all the pipes and hogsheads and casks in the cellar went rocking backwards and forwards with so much force that he thought every one would have been staved in and that he should have been drowned in wine.

When Jack Leary recovered, he made his way back to the dining room, where he found his master and the company very impatient for his return.

"What kept you?" said Mr. Mac Carthy in an angry voice, "and where is the wine? I rang for it half an hour ago!"

"The wine is in the cellar, I hope, sir," said Jack, trembling violently, "and I hope 'tis not all lost."

"What do you mean, fool?" roared Mr. Mac Carthy, "Why did you not fetch some with you?"

Jack Leary looked wildly about him, and only uttered a deep groan.

"Gentlemen," said Mr. Mac Carthy to his guests, "this is too much. When I next invite you to dinner, I hope it will be in another house, for I can no longer remain in this one, where a man has no command over his own wine cellar, and cannot get a butler to do his duty. I have long thought of moving from Ballinacarthy, and I am now determined, with the blessing of God, to depart it tomorrow. But wine shall you have if I myself must go to the cellar for it." Thus having spoken, he rose from his table, took the key and lantern from poor Jack Leary, and descended the narrow stairs to his cellar.

When he arrived at the door, which he found open, he thought he heard a noise, as if rats or mice were scrambling over the casks, and advancing a few steps further, he saw a little figure, about six inches in height, seated astride upon the pipe of the oldest port in the place, and bearing a spigot upon his shoulder. Raising the lantern, Mr. Mac Carthy contemplated the little fellow with wonder: he wore a red night-cap upon his head, round about him was a short leather apron, and his stockings were of a light blue color, so long as nearly to cover the entire of his leg, with huge silver buckles in his shoes, and high heels—out of vanity to make him appear taller. His face was like a withered winter apple, and his nose, which was a bright crimson, wore a delicate purple bloom about the tip, like that of a plum, yet his eyes twinkled, and his mouth twitched up at one side with an arch grin.

"Ha, scoundrel!" exclaimed Mr. Mac Carthy, "have I found you at last? Disturber of my cellar—what are you doing here?"

"Sure, and master," returned the little fellow, looking up at him with one eye, and with the other throwing a sly glance toward the spigot on his shoulder, "are we not moving tomorrow, and sure you would not leave your own little Cluricaune Naggeneen behind you?"

"Oh!" said Mr. Mac Carthy, "if you are to follow me, master Naggeneen, I don't see much use in quitting Ballinacarthy." So, filling with wine the basket which young Jack Leary in his fright had left behind him, and locking the cellar door, he rejoined his guests.

For some years after, Mr. Mac Carthy had always to fetch the wine from his table himself, as little Cluricaune Naggeneen seemed to feel a personal respect toward him. Notwithstanding this hard labor, the lord of Ballinacarthy lived in his paternal mansion to a good round age, and was famous to the last for the excellence of his wine and the conviviality of his company. Alas, by the time of his death, that same conviviality had nearly emptied the wine cellar, and as it was never so well filled again, nor so often visited, the revels of Naggeneen became less celebrated, and are now only spoken of in the legends of the country. It is even said that the poor little fellow took the decline of the cellar so to heart that he became negligent and careless of himself, and that he has even been sometimes seen going about with hardly a *skreed* to cover him. ❧

The Demon Cat

Jn Connemara, there was a wife of a fisherman, whose husband always had good luck with fishing. She was never short of fish in her kitchen and she always had plenty of fish to take to the market. She enjoyed her husband's good fortune, until she discovered that a great cat had been entering her home at night and devouring all the best fish in the house. So she decided to keep a close watch over her home at night with a big stick by her side.

One late afternoon, she and her friend were at work spinning when the house suddenly became dark and the front door burst open. A huge black cat walked into the room and went straight to the hearth. He then turned and growled at the two ladies.

"This can only be the devil," responded the young woman who was there with the fisherman's wife.

"Call me the devil, will you?" growled the cat. He then jumped towards the young woman and scratched at her arms and legs until both were left bleeding badly. "Now, maybe you will treat me with a little more respect when a gentleman like myself comes to visit you." He then walked over to the door, and shut it hard and stood before it so that neither of the two women could escape. The young woman began crying and sobbing from the pain of her arms and legs and from her fear of the cat.

A man happened to be walking by and heard the cries. He tried to get in through the front door, but found it was blocked. With much force, he pushed open the door, and found the cat standing there. So he took a large stick and pummeled the cat with a few good blows. The cat reeled back some, but then returned the blows with many scratches to the man's face and hands. The man, quickly realizing the strength of the cat, ran away as swiftly as he could.

Pleased with himself, the cat responded, "Now, let's eat! I wonder what the fisherman has caught recently. Hm, let's see…" said the cat as he approached the table filled with all sorts of splendid fish. He picked up some of the best fish on the table and quickly devoured them.

"Get out of here, you wicked cat," the woman cried. She hit the cat hard with a pair of tongs, but as the cat was the devil, he only turned around and grinned at her.

The cat continued to eat all the best fish he could get his paws on. Watching this, the women could take no more. They decided to make another attack on this beastly cat, so they rushed at him with knives and sticks and clobbered him hard enough to kill him. But the cat only turned around and blew fire from his mouth and tore at their heads with his large claws, drawing blood with every scratch. The women could take no more, and ran out of the house screaming at the top of their lungs.

Now an old lady happened to being passing by when she heard the screams of the two women. Curious, she looked into the house and saw the cat devouring the fish. The cat looked quite evil, so the old lady brought out a bottle of holy water from her pouch and quietly approached the cat. With a few quick sprinkles, the cat was soon covered with the old woman's holy water. The cat let out a wretched cry and burst into a large cloud of black smoke that filled the room. When the smoke had cleared, all that was left of the cat were his two red eyes burning like hot coals and the fur of his skin which shrivelled up into a ball and quickly turned into ashes.

No longer was the fisherman's wife bothered again by the power of the Evil One. The fish remained plentiful and untouched and the Demon Cat never appeared again.

The Black Hole of Knockfierna

Once upon a time there lived a strapping young fellow out of Connaught named Carroll O'Daly, who was known in his own country as "Devil Daly."

Carroll O'Daly used to go roving about from one place to another, and the fear of nothing stopped him. He would as soon pass an old churchyard or a regular fairy ground, at any hour of the night, as go from one room into another, without ever making the sign of the cross, or saying "Good luck attend you, gentlemen."

It so happened that he was once journeying in the county of Limerick, towards "The Balbec of Ireland," the venerable town of Kilmallock. Just at the foot of Knockfierna he overtook a respectable-looking man jogging along upon a white pony. The night was coming on, and they rode side by side for some time. Not much conversation passed between them further than saluting each other very kindly. At last, Carroll O'Daly asked his companion how far he was going.

"Not much further," said the farmer, for so he was dressed. "I'm only going to the top of this hill."

"And what might take you there," asked O'Daly, "at this time of night?"

"Why then," replied the farmer, "if you want to know, 'tis the Good People."

"The fairies, you mean," said O'Daly.

"Shhhh! quiet!" whispered his fellow traveler, "or you may be sorry for it," and he turned his pony off the road towards a little path that led up the side of the mountain. He wished Carroll O'Daly a good night and a safe journey.

"That fellow," thought Carroll, "is about no good tonight. I would swear my Bible oath that it is something else besides the fairies, or the Good People as he calls them, that is taking him up the mountain at this hour. The fairies!" he repeated. "Why would a strong man like him be going after little chaps like the fairies? To be sure, some say there are such things, and more say not. But I do know this—I wouldn't be afraid of a dozen fairies, or two dozen, for that matter, if they are no bigger than what I've heard."

Carroll O'Daly, while thinking of the Little People, had fixed his eyes steadfastly on the mountain, behind which the full moon was rising majestically. Upon an elevated point that appeared darkly against the moon's disk, he beheld the figure of a man leading a pony, and he had no doubt it was that of the farmer with whom he had just parted company.

A sudden urge to follow him flashed across O'Daly's mind with the speed of lightning—both his courage and curiosity had been worked up by these mysterious fairies. And muttering "Here's after you, old boy," he jumped from his horse, tethered him to an old-thorn tree, and started up the trail!

He followed as best he could the direction taken by the man and the pony, sometimes guided by glimpses of them ahead. After climbing for nearly three hours along a rugged and sometimes swampy path, he came to a green glade on top of the mountain, where he saw the white pony grazing freely, as quietly as might be. O'Daly looked around for the rider, but he was nowhere to be seen.

However, nearby the pony he did discover an opening in the mountain like the mouth of a pit, and he remembered a tale about the "Poul-duve" or Black Hole of Knockfierna. According to the story, the Black Hole was the entrance to the fairy castle which was deep inside the mountain. The legend told of a man named Ahern, a land surveyor in that part of the country, who had once attempted to fathom its depth with a line, but had been drawn down into the hole and never heard from again!

"But," thought O'Daly, "these are old women's stories, and since I've come so far, I'll just knock at the castle door and see if the fairies are home."

No sooner said than done. And seizing a large stone bigger than his two hands, he flung it with all his strength down into the Poul-duve of Knockfierna. He heard it bounding and tumbling about from one rock to another with a terrible noise. He leaned his head over to try and hear if it would reach the bottom, when what came flying out of the hole but the very same stone he had thrown in. It hurtled out of the hole with as much force as it had when falling down and gave O'Daly such a blow full in the face that it sent him rolling down the side of Knockfierna, head over heels, tumbling from one crag to another, falling much faster then he had climbed up.

In the morning Carroll O'Daly was found lying beside his horse. The bridge of his nose was badly broken (an injury that would disfigure him for life), his head was cut and bruised, and both his eyes were swollen closed and blackened.

Carroll O'Daly was never again bold in his rides alone at dusk near the haunts of the fairies, but small blame to him for that. And if ever he happened to be riding at night in a lonesome place, he would make the best of his way to the journey's end without asking questions or turning to the right or to the left, for fear of meeting once more the Good People, or any who kept company with them. ❧

Conan mac Morna

There was once a man called Conan mac Morna. He was big and bald and unwieldy in manly exercises, but his tongue was bitter and scurrilous. No brave deed was done that Conan the Bald did not mock and belittle. It is said that when he was stripped he showed down his back and buttocks a black sheep's fleece instead of a man's skin, and this is the way it came about.

One day when Conan was hunting in the forest along with other members of the Fianna, they came to a stately *dūn*, white-walled, with colored thatching on the roof. The men entered it to seek hospitality and found no one there—only a great, empty hall with pillars of cedar-wood and silken hangings like the hall of a wealthy lord. There was a table set with a sumptuous feast of boar's flesh and venison, red wine, and cups of gold and silver. So they sat down and ate and drank gaily until one of them jumped up to his feet with a cry of fear. The others looked around and saw before their eyes the tapestried walls changing to rough wooden beams and the ceiling to a foul, sooty thatch like that of a herdsman's hut. So they knew they were being entrapped by some enchantment of the Fairy Folk.

Everyone sprang to their feet and ran to the door, which was no longer high and stately, but was shrinking to the size of a fox warren. However, Conan the Bald remained; gluttonously devouring the good things on the table, and heeded nothing else. His colleagues shouted to him as the last of them went out. When Conan strove to rise and follow, he found himself limed to the chair so that he could not stir. Two of the Fianna, seeing his plight, rushed back and seized his arms and tugged with all their might. As the men dragged him away they left part of his clothing and his skin sticking to the chair. Then, not knowing what else to do with him in his sore plight, they clapped upon his back the nearest thing they could find, which was the skin of a black sheep that they took from a peasant's flock nearby. The skin grew there and Conan wore it till his death.

The Great Mr. Barry of Cairn Thierna

Though clean and pretty today, Fermoy was once like so many other villages in the past, a dirty and ugly place. Back then, there were no barracks, churches, or schools. The few two-storied houses along the street were mostly surrounded by rows and rows of pitiful mud shacks.

One day, a military regiment was moving from Dublin and Cork on foot. One company was to hike the troublesome march from Caher in the morning to Fermoy late in the evening after passing through a number of other towns and over a few mountains. As no barracks were there to house the soldiers, the company was soon calling out for the name and residence of the billet-master.

"Do you want Mr. Consadine?" answered one villager.

"How are we supposed to answer you when all you soldiers are asking the same thing all at once?" asked another.

"Poor lot the whole of them," said a third villager, "they don't do anything but eat all our food without even a thanks."

"Hey, watch it," said his neighbor, pushing aside the last speaker, "if you're looking for the billet-master's house, it is over there at the end of the road, with the light by the front door."

"Aye, that sounds like an honest man," replied a soldier, "we'll follow you down to his house." So off the villager went, with all the men of war close behind.

The billet-master, Mr. Consadine, was a man of some importance in Fermoy. He was stocky, and moved with a slow deliberate step that in some way reflected his public standing in the village. He was never without some showing of linen between his waistband and waistcoat and his breech-pockets were never buttoned. He also never wore any cravat and never buttoned the top button of his shirt so as to display the bull-like proportions of his neck and chest. A flaxen bob-wig decorated his head and behind his ear was stuck an *ex-officio* pen. Billet-master-general, barony sub-constable, and deputy clerk of the session constituted Mr. Consadine's standing in the community.

He was hard at work when Ned Flynn knocked. His maid answered the door, when the next thing Mr. Consadine heard was Ned cry out, "Sir, the soldiers are here! Can't you hear them?"

"It's best not to welcome at this hour, Mr. Flynn," Mr.

Consadine responded as he prepared himself to get back to work at his desk.

First, the officers were sent in, with the sergeants and corporals being billeted to those households indifferent to Mr. Consadine, as he considered himself a worthy man, he didn't want to bother his best friends if he could help it.

Soon after all the other soldiers had been sent off to their quarters, one poor fellow, who had fallen asleep leaning on his musket, woke up startled to see that nearly everyone had departed. He rushed over to Mr. Consadine, who just then was getting ready to leave. As he was late in requesting a billet, the young soldier begged Mr. Consadine a good lodging.

"Is that what you wish, young man," said the billet-master-general, barony sub-constable, and deputy-clerk. "Well, let's see what I can do. Ah, here we are. You shall sleep tonight in the largest house in Fermoy. For I am going to make out a billet for you upon Mr. Barry of Cairn Thierna."

"Thank you, sir," the soldier kindly replied.

"Yes, Mr. Barry of Cairn Thierna, the owner of the grandest house in this part of the country," triumphed Dick Consadine. "Here, just let me write out the billet."

After thanking the billet-master-general, barony sub-constable, and deputy-clerk, the young soldier packed up his knapsack and musket and left the office.

As he saw the soldier depart for the darkest part of town, Mr. Consadine let go a chuckle over the trick he played on the soldier, and a laugh at the thought of someone trying to find Barry of Cairn Thierna's house. Well, didn't he tell the truth, he asked himself. Was there any grander home than that of Mr. Barry's, whose roof was the blue vault of the sky and whose floor covered the mountain tops? For Barry of Cairn Thierna was one of the ancient chieftains of old who had become enchanted on the mountain of Cairn Thierna, where he would every so often be seen by a farmer.

The soldier was told that Mr. Barry lived outside of town on Cork road, but no matter where the soldier looked he could only see the dark mountains of Cairn Thierna.

After a long while, he finally met a man whom he could ask about the grand house of Mr. Barry.

"Well, and what Mr. Barry would that be?" asked the man.

"I'm not exactly sure. Your billet-master, Mr. What's-his-name, gave me directions, but in this dark, I can't see a thing," the soldier said. "He said it was a grand house, and he referred to the owner as the great Mr. Barry."

"Aye," answered the man, "that wouldn't be the great Barry of Cairn Thierna would it?"

"That's it," responded the soldier, "can you tell me where I can find Mr. Barry's house?"

"The great Barry of Cairn Thierna—I'll tell you where it's at, but I never heard of any soldier being billeted to spend a night in that place I tell you," cried the man. "It seems mighty strange to me. Look up, see that mountain there, that's Cairn Thierna. Now Mr. Barry's place is at the very top of it. It's quite easy to spot once you're there."

The tired soldier gave a sigh of relief as he walked onwards, but he had not gone too far when he heard the galloping of hoofs approaching him. When the horse came into view, the soldier noticed a tall gentleman fellow on a royal gray horse. The first thing the soldier did was to ask the fellow about Mr. Barry of Cairn Thierna.

"I'm Barry of Cairn Thierna," replied the gentleman, "why do you ask?"

"Good sir, I've received a billet from Mr. Consadine on your house," said the soldier.

"So you do, do you," Mr. Barry answered, "well, it is close by. Follow me, and you'll be taken care of."

He turned the horse off the road and up a steep climb. The solider was quite surprised that the horse make this climb with little effort, when he was scrambling on his hands and knees. But when they got to the top, the soldier had little difficulty in recognizing Mr. Barry's house. It was the greatest house in the land. The building was three stories high, and with all the windows lit up, it looked as if there was a grand party in progress. The front door opened and a servant walked down the flight of stone steps to take the horse from his master and led it into one of the stables.

The soldier entered the house and to his surprise, Mr. Barry didn't send the soldier downstairs to spend the night in the cellar as many of the other residents of Fermoy would have done. Instead, he brought the soldier into the parlor and asked to see his billet.

The great Mr. Barry looked it over and smiled to himself. "I know this Dick Consadine quite well—he's a good-humored chap, and he possesses some of the finest cows in these parts," Mr. Barry said.

Then calling for some of his servants, Mr. Barry had them prepare the dinner table, fill their glasses with drink, and cook up a large, thick sirloin of beef for them both.

"Sit down," said Mr. Barry, "you must've had a long day. Let's enjoy this meal and thank the gods."

The young soldier couldn't believe that he could be so fortunate. What had he done to deserve such an honor as to receive a billet for the great Mr. Barry's home? The meal was excellent, the wine superb, and his immediate surroundings resounded with impeccable taste. Soon they retired to the fireplace.

They sat a long time talking over the punch by the fire. Mr. Barry was a true gentleman. He could talk knowingly on an infinite number of subjects. The soldier could have carried on like this all night, but the long day was getting the best of him. When his eyes started drooping, Mr. Barry recognized that it was time to prepare the young soldier's bed. Mr. Barry had his servants help the soldier from his armchair and assist him to his room for the night. The soldier said his thanks for the umpteenth time and was walking towards the door when Mr. Barry stopped him.

"See that bundle in the hallway," Mr. Barry replied, "it's the hide of the cow that supplied our excellent meal tonight. Could you please give it to the billet-master when you return to your troops tomorrow and tell him that Barry of Cairn Thierna sent it to him. He will know what's it about, so good night, young man, I'm afraid you'll not be seeing me in the morning as I must be off and on my way long before the sun rises."

After saying good night, the solider picked up the bundle and retired to his room fitted with a large bed and a pleasant view of the village of Fermoy down in the valley below.

The next morning the bright rays of the sun awoke him. He was lying on his side, when he saw a bee floating about a patch of wild flowers beside him. He looked up and saw the great blue sky overhead with a few birds singing in the tall trees to his left. He rubbed his eyes for there was no sight at all of Mr. Barry's splendid home. There was no roof overhead and no fine mattress underneath him. He was lying down in a small field at the top of Cairn Thierna with the leather bundle Mr. Barry had given him that he was now using for a pillow.

"What is this," questioned the soldier, "last night I was dining with Mr. Barry in a fine house with many servants, but now I find myself alone at the top of a mountain without a luxury nearby."

Now the soldier got up and after wrapping up the cow hide, he began his hike back down the mountain to the village of Fermoy where he would visit the billet-master first thing upon his arrival.

When he reached the village the first thing he did was to see Mr. Consadine. "Hello there, young soldier," Mr. Consadine greeted the young soldier. "How was your night with Mr. Barry of Cairn Thierna?"

"Excellent," replied the soldier. "We feasted on fine meat and the best of wines, and he also gave me this present to give to you. He said for you to take this cow hide so that you may have something by which you could remember him by."

"Well, give my thanks to Mr. Barry," said the billet-master with a slight smirk on his face. "I don't know where he got this skin, but a fine piece of cow hide it is."

Now Mr. Consadine was just finishing his sentence when he spotted his cow boy running up the street towards his office. "Mr. Consadine, Mr. Consadine, there's a cow missing from the herd, there's a cow missing from the herd!" the young cow boy exclaimed.

The young cow boy entered his office and saw the leather piece upon the soldier's shoulder.

"That's it, that's it, there's the hide from the missing cow!" shouted the cow boy. "I know it, there's the two white spots by her left ear, and there's the scratch where she rubbed against the barbed wire fence."

"You're quite right," said the billet-master, "I have no doubt that it was the great Barry of Cairn Thierna who killed my best cow, and who has left me this hide as a reminder of his overseeing power. Well, this will be a warning for Dick Consadine never again to play tricks on travelers."

The Little Weaver

Once there lived a weaver in the town of Duleek, and by all accounts he was a very honest and industrious man. One morning his housekeeper called to him as he was sitting and throwing the shuttle.

She said, "Your brekquest is ready!"

"Lave me alone," he said, "I'm busy with a patthern here that is brakin' my heart, and until I complate and masther it intirely I won't quit."

"Oh, think o' the iligant stirabout that'll be spylte intirely."

"To the divil with the stirabout!" he said.

"God forgive you," she said, "for cursin' your good brekquest."

When he did finally leave the loom and went over to the stirabout he found it as black as a crow. Being that it was the height of summer the flies had lit upon it and the stirabout was fairly covered with them.

"Well, thin, bad luck to your impidence," said the weaver. "Would no place sarve you but that? And is it spyling my brekquest yiz are, you dirty bastes?"

And with that being all out of the temper at the time, he lifted his hand, and made one great slam at the disk of stirabout and killed no less than three score and ten flies at the one blow. It was three score and ten exactly, for he counted the carcasses one by one, and laid them out on a clean plate to view them.

He felt a powerful spirit rising within him when he saw the slaughter he had done at one blow, and with that he got as conceited as the very dickens. Not a stroke more work did he do that day, but out he went being fractious and impudent to everyone he met.

He went squaring up to their faces saying, "Look at that fist! That's the fist that killed three score and tin at one blow. Whoo! It is throwin' away my time I have been all my life stuck to my loom, nothin' but a poor waiver, when it is Saint George or the Dhraggin I ought to be, which is two of the sivin champions o' Christendom. I'm determined on it, and I'll set off immediately and be a knight arriant."

The next day he went about to his neighbors and got an old kettle from one and a saucepan from another, and he took them to the tailor. The tailor sewed him up a suit of tin clothes like any knight errant, and the weaver borrowed a pot lid. He was very particular about the lid since it was to be his shield. He went to a friend of his

who was a painter and a glazier, and made him paint on
his shield in big letters:

I'M THE MAN OF ALL MIN,
THAT KILL'D THREE SCORE AND TIN
AT A BLOW

"When the people sees that," said the weaver to himself, "the sorra one will dar for to come near me."

And with that he told the housekeeper to scour out the
small iron pot for him, "for," he said, "it will make an iligant helmet."

And when it was done he put it on his head and she
said, "Is it puttin' a great heavy iron pot an your head
you are by way iv a hat?"

"Sartinly," he said, "for a knight arriant should always
have a woight an his brain."

"But" said she, "there's a hole in it, and it can't keep
out the weather."

"It will be cooler," he said, putting it on him. "Besides,
if I don't like it, it is aisy to stop it with a wisp o' sthraw,
or the like o' that."

"The three legs of it looks mighty quare stickin' up,"
said she.

"Every helmet has a spike stickin' out o' the top of it,"
said the weaver, "and if mine has three, it's only the grand-
her it is."

"Well," said the housekeeper, getting bitter at last, "all
I can say is, it isn't the first sheep's head was dhress'd
in it."

"Your sarvint, ma'am," he said, and off he set.

He was in want of a horse, and so he went to a field by

where the miller's horse that used to carry the ground corn around the country was grazing.

"This is just the horse for me," said the weaver. "He is used to carryin' flour and male, and what am I but the flower o' shovelry in a coat o' mail. So the horse won't be put out iv his way in the laste."

But as he was riding the horse off the field, who should see him but the miller.

"Is it stalin' my horse you are, honest man?" said the miller.

"No," said the weaver, "I'm only goin' to axercise him in the cool o' the evenin' it will be good for his health."

"Thank you kindly," said the miller, "but lave him where he is, and you'll obleege me."

"I can't afford it," said the weaver, running the horse at the ditch.

"Bad luck to your impidence," said the miller. "You've as much tin about you as a thravelin' tinker, but you've more brass. Come back here, you vagabone!"

But he was too late—away galloped the weaver taking the road to Dublin, for he thought the best thing he could do was to go to the King of Dublin, and he thought maybe the King of Dublin would give him work. When he got to Dublin he went straight to the palace, and when he got into the courtyard he let his horse go and graze about the place.

The King was looking out of his drawing room window for diversion when the weaver came in. But the weaver pretended not to see him, and he went over to a stone seat under the window feigning sleep. However, he took care to turn out the front of his shield that had the letters on it.

When the King saw the sign he called out to one of the lords, "Look here, what do you think of a vagabone like that comin' undher my very nose to go sleep? It is thrue I'm a good King and I 'commodate the people by havin' sates for them to sit down and enjoy the raycreation and contimplation of seein' me here lookin' out o' my dhrawin'-room windy for divarshin—but that is no rayson they are to make a hotel o' the place and come and sleep here. Who is it at all?" said the King.

"Not a one o' me know, plaze your majesty," answered the lord.

"I think he must be a furriner," said the King, "bekase his dhress is outlandish."

"And doesn't know manners, more betoken," said the lord.

"I'll go down and circumspect him myself," said the King. "Folly me."

Down he went, followed by the lord, and when he went over to where the weaver was lying the first thing he saw was his shield with the big letters on it.

"By dad, this is the very man I want," said the King.

"For what, plaze your majesty?" asked the lord.

"To kill that vagabone dhraggin, to be sure," said the King.

"Sure, do you think he could kill him," said the lord, "when all the stoutest knights in the land wasn't aiquil to it, but never kem back, and was ate up alive by the cruel desaiver."

"Sure, don't you see there," said the King, pointing at the shield, "that he killed three score and tin at one blow. And the man that done that, I think is a match for anything."

So, with that, he went over to the weaver and shook him by the shoulder to wake him, and the weaver rubbed his eyes as if he had just awakened.

"God save you!" said the King.

"God save you kindly!" said the weaver, pretending not to know who he was speaking to.

"Do you know who I am" said the King, "that you make so free, good man?"

"No, indeed," said the weaver. "You have the advantage o' me."

"To be sure I have" said the King, mighty high, "sure ain't I the King o' Dublin?"

The weaver dropped down on his two knees in front of the King and said, "I beg God's pardon and yours for the liberty I tuk; plaze your holiness, I hope you'll excuse it."

"No offince," said the King. "Get up, good man. And what brings you here?"

"I'm in want o' work, plaze your riverence," said the waiver.

"Well, suppose I give you work?" said the King.

"I'll be proud to sarve you, my lord," said the weaver.

"Very well," said the King. "You killed three score and tin at one blow, I understan'."

"Yiz," said the weaver, "that was the last thrifle o' work I done, and I'm afeared my hand 'ill go out o' practice if I don't get some job to do at wanst."

"You shall have a job immediately. It is not three score and tin, or any fine thing like that. It is only a blaguard dhraggin that is disturbin' the counthry and ruinatin' my tinathry wid atin' their powlthry, and I'm lost for want of eggs," said the King.

"Troth, thin, plaze your worship," said the weaver, "you look as yellow as if you swallowed twelve yolks this minit."

"Well, I want this dhraggin to be killed," said the King. "It will be no throuble in life to you, and I'm only sorry that it isn't betther worth your while, for he isn't worth fearin' at all. Only I must tell you that he lives in the county Galway, in the middle of a bog, and he has an advantage in that."

"Oh, I don't value it in the laste," said the weaver, "for the last three score and tin I killed was in a soft place."

"When will you undhertake the job, then?" asked the King.

"Let me at him at wanst," said the weaver.

"That's what I like," said the King. "You're the very man for my money."

"Talkin' of money," said the weaver, "by the same token, I'll want a thrifle o' change from you for my thravellin' charges."

"As much as you plaze," said the King.

He immediately brought the weaver into his closet where there was an old stocking in an oak chest bursting with gold guineas.

"Take as many as you plaze," said the King.

The little weaver soon stuffed his tin clothes as full as they could hold of the gold guineas.

"Now I'm ready for the road," said the weaver.

"Very well," said the King. "But you must have a fresh horse."

"With all my heart," said the weaver who thought he might as well exchange the miller's old one for a better.

He was very happy now since he had no such notion to fight the dragon. All he intended was to steal the gold and ride back again to Duleek with his gains and a good horse. But as cute as the weaver was, the King was cuter still. The minute the weaver was mounted, the horse which was trained to follow a certain route, galloped right down to Galway.

For four days he traveled until at last the weaver saw a crowd of people running as if Old Nick was at their heels shouting a thousand murders and crying, "The dhraggin, the dhraggin!"

He couldn't stop the horse nor make him turn back, but away he pelted right toward the terrible beast that was coming up to them. The weaver had no time to lose so he threw himself off the horse and made to a tree and clambered up into it as nimble as a cat. Meanwhile the dragon came up in a powerful rage and devoured the horse and began to sniffle and scent about for the weaver.

He soon found him up in the tree and said, "In troth, you might as well come down out o' that for I'll have you as sure as eggs is mate."

"Divil a fut I'll go down," said the weaver.

"Sorra care I care," said the dragon, "for you're as good as ready money in my pocket this minit, for I'll lie und-her this tree and sooner or later you must fall to my share."

And sure enough he sat down and began to pick his teeth with his tail since he had such a heavy breakfast that morning, having eaten an entire village along with the horse. He got drowsy at last and fell asleep. But before he went to sleep he wound himself all around the tree, as a lady would wind a ribbon around her finger, so that the weaver could not escape.

The minute the weaver knew that the dragon was in a deep sleep he started to creep down the tree as cautious as a fox. He was nearly at the bottom when a thieving branch broke and down he fell right on top of the dragon. But he fell with his two legs right across the dragon's neck. He laid hold of the beast's ears and there he kept his grip for the dragon awoke and endeavored to bite him. But the weaver was behind his ears so he could not. So he tried to shake him off but though he shook all the scales on his body he could not turn the scale against the weaver.

"By the hokey, this is too bad intirely," said the dragon, "but if you won't let go, by the powers o' wildfire, I'll give you a ride that'll astonish your siven small sinuses, my boy."

And with that away he flew and made straight towards Dublin. But the weaver being on his neck was a great distress to him and he flew and flew until he came slap up against the palace of the King. But being blind with rage, he never saw it and knocked his brains out.

Good luck would have it that the King of Dublin was looking out of his drawing-room window for diversion that day and when he saw the weaver riding on the fiery dragon, he called out to his courtiers to come and see the show.

"By the podhers o' war, here comes the knight arriant," said the King, "ridin' the dhraggin that's all afire, and if he gets into the place, yiz must be ready wid the fire ingines for to put him out."

But when they saw the dragon fall outside they all ran downstairs and scampered in the palace yard to get a better view. By the time they got down the weaver had got off the dragon's neck and ran up to the King.

"Plaze your holiness, I did not think myself worthy of

killin' this facetious baste, so I brought him to yourself for to do him the honor of decripitation by your own royal five fingers. But I tamed him first before I allowed him the liberty for to dar' to appear in your royal prisince, and you'll oblige me if you just make your mark with your own hand upon the onruly baste's neck."

The King drew out his sword and took the head off the dirty brute as clean as a new pin. There was great rejoicing in the court that the dragon had been killed.

The King turned to the little weaver and said, "You are a knight arriant as it is, and so it would be of no use for to knight you over again, but I will make you a lord."

"Oh, Lord!" said the weaver, thunderstruck at his own good luck.

"I will," said the King. "And as you are the first man I ever heered tell of that rode a dhraggin, you shall be called Lord Mount Dhraggin. But this is not all I'll do for you. I'll give you my daughter, too, in marriage."

Now, that was nothing more than what he promised the weaver in his first promise. By all accounts the King's daughter was the greatest dragon that ever was seen. She even had the devil's own tongue and a beard a yard long which she pretended was put on her by way of a penance by Father Mulcahy, her confessor. But is was well known that this trait had been in the family for ages. ❧

The Chivalric Quest

Once upon a time, Kymon, a knight of King Arthur's court, had a strange and unfortunate adventure. Riding forth in search of some deed of chivalry to do, he came to a splendid castle, where he was hospitably received by twenty-four damsels, of whom the least lovely was more lovely than Guinevere, the wife of Arthur. With them was a noble lord, who, after Kymon had eaten, asked of his business.

Kymon replied, "I am seeking my match in combat."

The lord of the castle smiled, and bade him, "You should take the road up the valley and through a forest until you come to a glade with a mound in the midst of it. On the mound you will see a black man of huge stature with one foot and one eye, bearing a mighty club. He is the wood-ward of that forest and will have thousands of wild animals, stags, serpents, and what not, feeding around him. He will show you what you are in quest of."

Kymon followed the instructions and met the black man. The black man then directed him to where he would find a fountain under a great tree.

"By the side of it," he said, "will be a silver bowl on a slab of marble. You are to take the bowl and throw a handful of water on the slab. When a terrific storm of hail and thunder follows there will break forth an enchanting music of singing birds. A knight in black armor will then appear riding on a coal-black horse, with a black pennon upon his lance. And if you do not find trouble in that adventure, you need not seek it during the rest of your life."

Kymon did as he was bidden and the Black Knight soon appeared. Silently they set lance in rest and charged. Kymon was flung to the earth, while his enemy, not bestowing one glance upon him, passed the shaft of his lance through the rein of Kymon's horse and rode off with it in the direction he had come. Kymon went back on foot to the castle, where none asked him how he had sped, but they did give him a new horse on which he rode home to Caerleon.

Upon arriving at King Arthur's court he told the people his tale. Now there was a brave knight by the name of Owain who was, of course, fired by Kymon's adventure. The next morning at dawn of day he rode forth to seek for the same quest. All passed as it had done in Kymon's case, but Owain wounded the Black Knight so sorely that he turned his horse and fled. Owain pursued him hotly until they came to a vast and resplendent castle.

Across the drawbridge they rode, the outer portcullis of

which fell as the Black Knight passed it. But so close at his heels was Owain that the portcullis fell behind him, cutting his horse in two behind the saddle. He himself remained imprisoned between the outer gate of the drawbridge and the inner. While he was in this predicament a maiden came to him and gave him a ring.

She told him, "When you wear this ring with the stone reversed and clenched in your hand you will become invisible. When the servants of the lord of the castle come for you, elude them and follow me. I do this because I know of you—for as a friend you are the most sincere and as a lover the most devoted."

Owain did as he was bidden, and the maiden concealed him. That night a great lamentation was heard in the castle for the lord had died of the wound which Owain had given him. Soon afterwards Owain caught sight of the mistress of the castle and love of her took entire possession of him. Luned, the maiden who had rescued him, wooed her for him, and he became her husband, and lord of the castle of the Fountain and all the dominions of the Black Knight. He defended the fountain with lance and sword as his forerunner had done and made his defeated antagonists ransom themselves for great sums which he bestowed among his barons and knights. Thus he lived for three years.

After this time Arthur, with his nephew Gwalchmai and with Kymon for guide, rode forth at the head of an army to search for tidings of Owain. They came to the fountain and here they met Owain, neither knowing the other as their helmets were down. Kymon was overthrown quickly, and then Gwalchmai and Owain fought. After a while Gwalchmai was unhelmed.

Owain said, "My lord Gwalchmai, I did not know you. Take my sword and my arms."

Said Gwalchmai, "You, Owain, are the victor—you take my sword."

Arthur ended the contention in courtesy by taking the swords of both. Then they all rode to the Castle of the Fountain, where Owain entertained them with great joy. He soon went back with Arthur to Caerleon after promising his countess that he would remain there but three months and then return.

But at the Court of Arthur he forgot his love and his duty and remained there not three months but three years. At the end of that time a noble lady came riding upon a horse caparisoned with gold, and she sought out Owain and took the ring from his hand.

"Thus," she said, "shall be treated the deceiver, the traitor, the faithless, the disgraced, and the beardless."

Then she turned her horse's head and departed. And Owain, overwhelmed with shame and remorse, fled from the sight of men and lived in a desolate country with wild beasts until his body wasted and his hair grew long and his clothing rotted away.

When near to death from exposure and want, he was taken in by a certain widowed countess and her maidens, and restored to strength by magic balsams. Although they besought him to remain with them, he rode forth again, seeking for lonely and desert lands.

There he found a lion in battle with a great serpent. Owain slew the serpent, and the lion followed him and played about him as if it had been a greyhound that he had reared. By day it fed him by catching deer (Owain cooked part for himself while giving the rest to his lion to devour) and by night the beast kept watch over him.

As he continued on his journey, he found an imprisoned damsel, whose sighs he heard, though he could not see her nor she him.

"Who are you and why are you sighing?" he asked.

"My name is Luned, and I am the handmaid of a countess whose husband had left her. Her husband was the friend I loved best in the world. When two of the countess's pages had slandered his name, I defended him. But because I tried to protect him I was condemned to be burned within a year's time unless Owain, son of Urien, comes to deliver me before the year is out. But the year is to end tomorrow."

"I know that your friend will come to correct this insult," he said and departed.

On the next day Owain met the two youths leading Luned to execution, and with the help of the lion he overcame them and rescued her. They then returned to the Castle of the Fountain where Owain reconciled with his love and took her with him to Arthur's Court, and she was his wife there as long as she lived. ❦

The King of the Black Desert

When O'Connor was King of Ireland he had one son who grew up to be a wild young man and he would always have his own will in everything.

One morning the son went out a riding on his fine black horse, with his hound and his hawk by his side, singing a verse of song to himself, until he came as far as a big bush that was growing on the brink of a glen. There was a gray old man sitting at the foot of the bush, and he said, "King's son, if you are able to play as well as you are able to sing songs, I would like to play a game with you." The King's son thought this was a silly old man, and he alighted, threw bridle over branch, and sat down by his side.

The old man drew out a pack of cards and asked, "Can

you play these?"

"I can," said the King's son.

"What shall we play for?" said the gray old man.

"Anything you wish," answered the King's son.

"All right! If I win you must do for me anything I shall ask of you, and if you win I must do for you anything you ask of me," said the gray old man.

"I'm satisfied," said the King's son.

So they played the game and the King's son beat the gray old man. Then he said, "What would you like me to do for you, King's son?"

"I won't ask you to do anything for me. I think that you are not able to do much," replied the King's son.

"Don't mind that," said the old man. "You must ask me to do something. I never lost a bet that I wasn't able to pay."

The King's son was even more convinced that this was a silly old man and to satisfy him he said, "Take the head off my stepmother and put a goat's head on her for a week."

"I'll do that for you," said the gray old man.

The King's son rode off on his horse and he headed for another place without thinking again of the gray old man until he went home. When he arrived he found a great grief in the castle. The servants told him that an enchanter had put a goat's head on the Queen in place of her own.

"By my hand, but that's a wonderful thing," said the King's son. "If I had been at home I'd have whipt the head off him with my sword."

The King was very upset and he sent for a wise man and asked him if he knew how this could have happened to the Queen.

"Indeed, I cannot tell you that," he said, "it's a work of enchantment."

The King's son did not let on that he had any knowledge of the matter, but the following morning he went out a-riding on his fine black horse, with his hound and his hawk by his side, singing a verse of song to himself, and he never drew rein until he came as far as the big bush on the brink of the glen. There the gray old man was still sitting under the bush and he said, "King's son, will you have a game today?"

The King's son said, "I will." With that he threw bridle over branch and sat down beside the old man, who drew out the cards and asked the King's son if he got the thing he had won yesterday, and the King's son told him that he did.

"We'll play for the same bet today," said the gray old man.

"I'm satisfied," said the King's son.

They played and the King's son won.

"What would you like me to do for you this time?" asked the gray old man.

The King's son thought and said to himself, "I'll give him a hard job this time." Then he replied, "There's a field of seven acres at the back of my father's castle, let it be filled tomorrow morning with cows, and no two of them to be of one color, or one height, or one age."

"That shall be done," said the gray old man.

And the King's son went riding off on his horse and faced for home, where he found the King still sorrowful about the Queen, since no doctor in Ireland could do her any good.

The next morning the King's herdsman went out early

and he saw that the field at the back of the castle was filled with cows, of which no two were of the same color, height, or age. He went in and told the King of the wonderful news.

"Go and drive them out," said the King. The herdsman tried but no sooner would he put them out on one side than they would come in on the other. He went to the King again and told him that all the men in Ireland would not be able to put out these cows.

"They must be enchanted cows," said the King.

When the King's son saw the cows, he said to himself, "I'll have another game with the gray old man today!"

That morning he went out a riding on his fine black horse, with his hound and his hawk by his side, singing a verse of song to himself, and he never drew rein till he came to the bush on the brink of the glen. The gray old man was there and asked him if he would play a game of cards.

"I will," said the King's son, "but you know well that I can beat you playing cards."

"We'll play another game. Did you ever play ball?" asked the old man.

"I did indeed," said the King's son, "but I think that you are too old to play ball, and besides that, we have no place to play."

"If you are contented to play I will find a place," answered the gray old man.

"I'm contented," said the King's son.

"Follow me," said the gray old man.

The King's son followed him through the glen until he came to a green hill. There he drew out a little enchanted rod and spoke some words which the King's son did not understand. After a moment, the hill opened and the two men went in. They passed through splendid halls and came out into a wonderful garden with a place for playing ball. They threw up a piece of silver to see who would have hand-in, and the gray old man got it.

They began to play and the gray old man quickly won the game. The King's son asked the old man what he would like him to do.

"I am King over the Black Desert. You must find me and my dwelling place within a year and a day or I shall find you and you shall lose your head," said the gray old man, and he brought the King's son out the same way they came in. The green hill closed behind them and the gray old man disappeared.

The King's son went home, a-riding on his horse, and he was very sorrowful.

That evening the King noticed his son was very troubled and heard his sighs and moans throughout the night. The next morning his son told him the whole story from beginning to end. Then the King sent for a wise man and asked if he knew where the King of the Black Desert lived.

"I do not indeed," said he, "but as sure as there's a tail on the cat, unless the young heir finds out, he will lose his head." There was great grief in the castle that day. The King's son was going searching for an enchanter without knowing whether he would ever come back.

After a week the goat's head was taken off the Queen and her own head was put upon her. When she heard of how the goat's head was put upon her, a great hate came upon her against the King's son and she voiced her desire that he might never come back, alive or dead.

The King's son left with the blessing of his father and all

his kindred. His traveling bag was packed, and he went a-riding on his fine black horse, with his hound and his hawk by his side, singing a verse of song to himself. He traveled until the sun went down and then searched for lodging. He noticed a large wood on his left-hand side and he drew toward it quickly, hoping to spend the night under the shelter of the trees. He sat down at the foot of a large oak tree and opened his traveling bag to take some food and drink when he saw a great eagle coming towards him.

"Do not be afraid of me, King's son. I know you, you are the son of O'Connor, King of Ireland. I am a friend, and if you give me your horse to feed my four hungry birds I shall carry you farther than your horse ever could, and perhaps I will put you on the track of him you are looking for."

"You can have the horse," said the King's son, "although I'm sorrowful at parting from him."

"All right, I shall be here tomorrow at sunrise." With that she opened her great gob, caught hold of the horse, and disappeared out of sight.

The King's son ate and drank his fill. It was not long before he fell asleep and did not stir until the eagle returned.

"It is time for us to be going, there is a long journey ahead. Take hold of your bag and leap upon my back," said the eagle.

"But to my grief I must part from my hound and my hawk," said the King's son.

"Do not be grieved," she said, "they will be here when you come back."

Then he leaped up on her back and they took flight. She brought him across hills and hollows, over a great sea, and over woods, until he thought he must be at the end of the world. They landed in the midst of a great desert and she said to him, "Follow the path on your right-hand side and it will bring you to the house of a friend. I must leave you now to feed my birds." And she was gone.

He followed the path and it was not long till he came to the house. There was a gray old man sitting in the corner. He rose and said, "A hundred thousand welcomes to you, King's son, from Rathcroghan of Connacht."

"I do not know you," said the King's son.

"I was acquainted with your grandfather," said the gray old man. "Sit down, you must be hungry." After the old man's signal, two servants came and laid out a meal for the King's son.

"Eat and drink," said the old man, "it might be some time before you have such opportunity." The King's son thanked the old man.

"You are looking for the King of the Black Desert," said the old man, "go to sleep now and I will go through my books to see if I can find out the dwelling place of that King."

The next morning the old man woke the King's son, gave him plenty to eat and drink, and a horse for his journey. He also gave him a little white garron and said, "Give the garron his head, and when he stops look up into the air. You will see three swans as white as snow. Those are the three daughters of the King of the Black Desert. There will be a green napkin in the mouth of one of them, that is the youngest daughter. She is the only one alive who can bring you to the house of the King of the Black Desert. When the garron stops you will be near a lake. The three swans will land on the brink of that lake, and they will make three young women of themselves. They will go into the lake swimming and dancing. Keep your eye on the green napkin and when the women are in the lake, go and get it. Hold on to it and do not let it go. Hide behind a tree and when the three women come out of the lake, two of them will turn into swans and fly away. The third will remain, and she will say, 'I will do anything for him who will give me my napkin back.' Give her the napkin and tell her there is nothing she can do except bring you to her father's house. Tell her you are the son of a King from a powerful country."

The King's son did everything just as the old man instructed. When he gave the napkin back to the daughter of the King of the Black Desert, he said, "I am the son of O'Connor, King of Connacht. Bring me to your father."

"Would it not be better for me to do something else for you?" she asked.

"I do not want anything else," he said.

"If I show you the house, will you be satisfied?" she asked.

"I will," he said.

"Now, upon your life do not tell my father that it was I who brought you to his house, and I shall be a good friend to you," she instructed.

"I will do as you say," he said.

Then she turned into a swan and said, "Leap up on my back, put your hands under my neck, and hold on tight."

He did this and they flew away, over glens, over seas, and over mountains. When they landed she asked him, "Do you see that great house yonder? That is my father's house. Anytime that you are in danger, I shall be at your side." Then she flew away.

The King's son went to the house and found the gray

old man sitting in a golden chair.

"King's son," he said, "I see that you have found me before the day and the year. How long since you have left home?"

"This morning, when I was rising out of my bed, I saw a rainbow. I gave a leap, spread my two legs on it, and slid as far as this," said the King's son.

"By my hand, it is a great feat you performed," said the old King.

"I could do a more wonderful thing than that if I chose," said the King's son.

"I have three things for you to do," said the old King, "and if you are able to do them, you shall have the choice of my three daughters for a wife, and unless you are able to do them you shall lose your head, as a good many other young men have lost it before you."

"Then," he said, "there will be neither eating or drinking in my house except once a week and we had it this morning."

"It's fine with me," replied the King's son, "I could fast for a month if I were in a pinch."

"No doubt you can go without sleep also," said the old King.

"I can, without a doubt," said the King's son.

"You shall have a hard bed tonight, then," said the old King. "Come with me and I shall show you." They went outside and the old King showed him a great tree with a fork in it, and said "Get up there and sleep in the fork, and be ready with the rise of the sun."

He went up into the fork, but as soon as the old King was asleep the young daughter came and brought him into a fine room, and kept him there until the old King was about to rise. Then she put him out again into the fork of the tree.

With the rise of the sun the old King came out and said, "Come down now and I will show you the thing that you have to do today."

He brought the King's son to the brink of a lake and showed him an old castle, and said, "Throw every stone in that castle out into the loch, and have it done before the sun goes down in the evening." And the old King left him.

The King's son began working, but the stones were stuck to one another so that he was not able to raise one of them. If he worked for days he thought he could never complete the task. He sat down and thought about what he could do. It was not long before the daughter of the old King came to him and asked, "What is the cause of your grief?" He told her the work which he had to do. "Let that put no grief on you, I will do it," she said. Then she gave him bread, meat, and wine, pulled out a little enchanted rod, struck a blow on the old castle, and in a moment every stone was at the bottom of the lake. "Now," she said, "do not tell my father that it was I who did the work for you."

When the sun went down in the evening, the old King came and said, "I see that you have your day's work done."

"I have," replied the King's son, "I can do any work at all."

The old King thought now that the King's son had great powers of enchantment, and he said to him, "Your day's work for tomorrow is to lift the stones out of the loch and set up the castle as it was before."

He brought the King's son home and said to him, "Go to sleep in the place you were last night."

When the old King went to sleep the young daughter came and brought him into the fine chamber, and kept him there till the old King was about to rise in the morning. Then she put him out again in the fork of the tree.

At sunrise the old King came and said, "It's time for you to get to work."

"There's no hurry," replied the King's son, "because I know I can readily do my day's work."

He then went to the brink of the lake, but he was not able to see a single stone because the water was black. He sat down on a rock, and it was not long until Finnuala, the old King's daughter, came to see him. "Let there be no grief on you. I can do that work for you," she said. Then she gave him bread, beef, and wine. After that she drew out the little enchanted rod, smote the water of the lake with it, and in a moment the old castle was set up as it had been the day before. Then she said to him, "On your life, don't tell my father that I did this work for you, or that you have any knowledge of me at all."

That evening the old King came and said, "I see that you have the day's work done."

"I have," said the King's son, "that was an easy job."

Then the old King thought that the King's son had more power of enchantment than he had himself. He said, "You have only one other thing to do." He brought him home and put him to sleep in the fork of the tree. Again, Finnuala came and put him into the fine chamber, and in the morning she sent him out again into the tree. At sunrise the old King came to him and said, "Come with me and I will show you your day's work."

He brought the King's son to a great glen and showed him a well. He said, "My grandmother lost a ring in that well, and you must find it for me before the sun goes down."

This well was one hundred feet deep and twenty feet round about, and it was filled with water, and there was an army out of hell watching the ring.

When the old King went away, Finnuala came and asked, "What have you to do today?" He told her and she said, "That is a difficult task, but I shall do my best to save your life." Then she gave him beef, bread, and wine. She made a diver of herself and went down into the well. It was not long before he saw smoke and lightning coming up out of the well, and he heard a sound like thunder.

When the smoke cleared, and the lightning and thunder stopped, Finnuala came up with the ring. She handed it to the King's son and said, "I won the battle, and your life is saved. But look, the little finger on my right hand is broken. But perhaps it's a lucky thing. When my father comes, do not give him the ring. Instead, threaten him. He will bring you, then, to choose your wife, and this is how you shall make your choice. I and my sisters will be in a room, there will be a hole in the door and we shall all put our hands out in a cluster. You will put your hand through the hole, and the hand that you keep hold of when my father opens the door will be the hand of your wife. You will know me by my broken little finger."

"I will do this, and the love of my heart you are, Finnuala," said the King's son.

That evening, the old King came and asked, "Did you get my grandmother's ring?"

"I did, indeed," said the King's son. "There was an army out of hell guarding it, but I beat them, and I would beat seven times as many. Don't you know I am a Connachtman?"

"Give me the ring," said the old King.

"Indeed, I won't give it," said the King's son. "I fought hard for it. But give me my wife so that I may be going."

The old King brought him in and said, "My three daughters are in that room before you. The hand of each of them is stretched out, and she on whom you will keep your hold until I open the door will be your wife."

The King's son thrust his hand through the hole in the door and caught hold of the hand with the broken little finger. He kept a tight hold of it until the old King opened the door.

"This is my wife," said the King's son. "Now give me your daughter's fortune."

"She has no fortune, only a brown, slender steed to bring you home. Go now and never come back, alive or dead!" cried the old King.

The King's son and Finnuala rode off on the brown, slender steed. When they came to the wood where the King's son left his hound and his hawk, they were there, waiting for him, along with his fine, black horse. He sent the brown, slender steed back and he and Finnuala went a-riding on his horse, together with his hound and his hawk, and they did not stop till they reached Rathcroghan. There was a great welcome for him there, and it was not long till he and Finnuala were married. ❧

Tom and the Princess Who Did Not Laugh

Long ago a poor, widowed woman lived down by the iron forge near Enniscorthy. She was so poor that she had no clothes to put on her son, Tom. So she used to leave him in the ash-hole, near the fire, and pile the warm ashes about him. Accordingly, as he grew up, she sunk the pit deeper and deeper. At last, by hook or by crook, she got a goatskin and fastened it around his waist. He felt quite grand. He ran outside and took his first walk down the street.

The next morning the lad's mother spoke to him.

"Tom, you thief, you've done no good for me yet, and you six feet tall and now past nineteen. Take that rope and bring me a log from the woods."

"Never say it twice, mother," said Tom, "I'm off."

He quickly gathered the firewood and was tying it up when what should suddenly come along but a big giant, nine feet high and swinging a club. Spry Tom jumped to one side and picked up a ram-pike. With his very first crack to the giant he knocked him to the ground.

"If you have a prayer to say," said Tom, "now's the time to pray it, before I make *brishe* of you."

"I have no prayers," said the giant, "but if you spare my life, I will give you my club. So long as you keep free from sin, you will win every battle you ever fight with it."

Tom made no bones about letting the giant go and eagerly reached for the club. As soon as he got the club in his hand he sat down on the log and gave it a tap with the log, saying, "Log, I had a great deal of trouble gathering you, and even ran the risk of my life for you. The least you can do is to carry me home." And sure enough, the wind of the word was all it took. The log went off through the woods, groaning and cracking till it reached the widow's door.

Well, when the firewood was all burned up Tom was sent off again to fetch more. This time he had to fight a giant with two heads on him. Tom had a little more trouble with him—that's all. And lacking any prayers, the *second* giant offered Tom a fife that made everyone dance to it when it was played. Tom accepted the enchanted fife and made the big giant dance all the way home, with Tom perched on his shoulders.

Now the next time Tom went to the woods to gather firewood for his mother, he met a giant with three heads. He fought and subdued this giant, too. This giant had no more prayers or catechism than the other two. Instead, he presented Tom with a bottle of green ointment that would protect the wearer against being burned, scalded, or wounded.

"And now," said the third giant, "there are no more of us. You may come and gather wood here till little *Lunacy Day* in harvest without giant or fairy man to disturb you."

Well now, Tom was prouder than ten peacocks, and it was his fashion to stroll down the street at the heel of the evening. But some of the little boys had no more manners than if they were Dublin *jackeens*, and put out their tongues to Tom's club and goatskin. He didn't like that at all, but knew it would be mean to give one of them a clout. At last, what should come through the town but a kind of bellman, only it's a big bugle he had instead of a bell, and a huntsman's cap on his head, and a kind of painted shirt. So this bugleman, if you will, proclaimed that the King of Dublin's daughter was so melancholy that she hadn't laughed for seven years, and that her father would grant her hand in marriage to whoever would make her laugh three times.

"That's the very thing for me to try," said Tom to himself, and so, without burning any more daylight, he kissed his mother good-bye, curled his club at the little boys, and set off along the high road to the town of Dublin.

At last Tom came to one of the city gates, but the guards laughed and cursed at him instead of letting him through. Tom stood it all for a little time, till at last one of them—out of fun, as he said—drove his bayonet half an inch or so into Tom's side. Tom did nothing but take the fellow by the scruff of his neck and the waistband of his corduroys and fling him in the canal. Some ran to pull the fellow out, and others to try to teach manners to the vulgarian with their swords and daggers. But a tap from his club sent them headlong into the moat or down on the stones, and they were soon begging him to stay his hand.

So finally one of them was glad enough to show Tom the way to the palace yard. And there were the King, the Queen, and the Princess in a gallery, looking at all sorts of wrestling and sword playing, long dances, and mumming, all to please the Princess. But not a smile came over her handsome face.

Well, they all stopped when they saw the young giant, with his boy's face and long black hair, and his short curly beard—for his poor mother couldn't afford to buy razors—and his great strong arms and bare legs, with no covering but the goatskin that reached from his waist to his knees. An envious wizened bastard of a fellow with red hair stepped forward. He, too, wished to be married to the Princess, and didn't like the way she looked at Tom. He demanded that Tom explain his business.

"My business," said Tom, "is to make the beautiful Princess, God bless her, laugh three times."

"Do you see all these merry fellows and skillful swordsmen," inquired the other, "that could eat you up with a grain of salt? Not a mother's soul of them has ever gotten a laugh from her these seven years."

So the fellows gathered around Tom, and the angry man aggravated him till he told them he didn't care a pinch of snuff for the whole lot of them. Let them come on six at time and try what they could do.

The King, who was too far off to hear what they were saying, asked what it was that the stranger wanted.

"He wants," said the red-haired fellow, "to make fools of your best men."

"Oh," said the King, "if that's the way it is, let one of them turn out and try the stranger's mettle."

So one stood forward, with sword and pot-lid, and made a cut at Tom. Tom struck the bold fellow's elbow with the club, and up over their heads flew the sword, and down went the owner of it on the gravel from a thump he got on the helmet. Another took his place, and another, and another, and then half a dozen at once, and Tom sent swords, helmets, shields, and bodies rolling over and over, and themselves bawling out that they were killed, and disabled, and damaged, and rubbing their poor elbows and hips, and limping away. Tom contrived not to kill anyone, and the Princess was so amused that she laughed a great sweet laugh that was heard all over the yard.

"King of Dublin," said Tom, "I've earned a quarter of your daughter."

And the King didn't know whether he was glad or sorry, and all the blood in the Princess's heart ran into her cheeks.

There was no more fighting that day, and Tom was invited to dine with the royal family. The next day Redhead told Tom of a wolf, the size of a yearling heifer, that used to saunter about the walls, eating people and cattle, and said what a pleasure it would give the King to have it killed.

"With all my heart," said Tom. "Send a *jackeen* to show me where he lives, and we'll see how he behaves to a stranger."

The Princess was not well pleased, for Tom looked a different person with fine clothes and a nice green beret over his long, curly hair. And besides, he had gotten one laugh out of her. However, the King gave his consent, and

in an hour and a half the horrible wolf was walking in
the palace yard, with Tom a step or two behind with his
club on his shoulder, just as a shepherd would walk after
a pet lamb. The King, Queen, and Princess were tucked
safely up in their gallery, but the officers and people of
the court were patroling about the great lawn. When they
saw the big beast coming they gave themselves up and
began to make for doors and gates. The wolf licked his
chops, as if he were saying, "Wouldn't I enjoy a breakfast of a couple of you!"

The King shouted out, "O Tom, take away that terrible
wolf, and you shall have all my daughter."

But Tom didn't mind him a bit. He pulled out his flute
and began to play like a vengeance and every man, woman,
and child in the yard began dancing away heel and toe.
The wolf himself was obliged to get on his hind legs and
dance "Tatther Jack Walsh" along with the rest. A good
deal of the people got inside and shut the doors so the
hairy fellow wouldn't pin them, but Tom kept playing,
and the outsiders kept shouting and dancing, and the
wolf kept dancing and roaring with the pain his legs were
giving him.

And all the while the wolf had his eyes on Redhead,
who was trapped in the yard along with the rest. Wherever
Redhead went the wolf followed, keeping one eye on him
and the other on Tom, to see if he would give him leave
to eat the troublemaker. But Tom shook his head, and
never stopped the tune, and Redhead never stopped dancing and bawling, nor the wolf dancing and roaring, one
leg up and the other down, ready to drop from standing
on his hind legs from fair tiresomeness.

When the Princess saw that there was no fear of anyone being killed she was so diverted by the stew that Redhead was in that she gave another great laugh.

"King of Dublin," cried Tom, "I now have two quarters of your daughter."

"Oh, quarters or all," said the King, "put away that devil of a wolf and we'll see about it."

So Tom put his flute in his pocket, and said he to the beast that was sitting on his *currabingo* ready to faint, "Walk off to the mountains, my fine fellow, and live like a respectable beast, and if ever I find you within seven miles of any town—" He said not more, but spit in his fist and gave a flourish of his club. It was all the poor devil wanted. He put his tail between his legs and took to his pumps without looking at man nor mortal; neither sun, moon, nor stars ever saw him in sight of Dublin again.

At dinner everyone laughed but the foxy fellow. Sure enough, he was laying out how he'd settle poor Tom the next day. "Well, to be sure!" said he, "King of Dublin you are in luck. There's the Danes murdering us to no end. If anyone can save us from 'em it is this gentleman with the goatskin. There is a flail hangin' on the collar-beam in Hell, and neither Dane nor Devil can stand before it."

"So," said Tom to the King, "will you let me have the other half of the Princess if I bring you the flail?"

"No, no," cried the Princess, "I'd rather never be your wife than see you in that danger."

But Redhead whispered and nudged Tom about how shabby it would look to renege on the adventure. So Tom asked him which way he was to go, and Redhead directed him through a street where a great many bad women lived, and a great many *shibbeen* houses were open, and away he set.

Well, he traveled and traveled till he came in sight of the walls of Hell. Before he knocked at the gates he carefully rubbed himself all over with the greenish ointment. When at last he knocked a hundred little imps popped their heads out through the bars and asked him what he wanted.

"I want to speak to the big Devil of All," said Tom, "open the gates!"

It wasn't long till the gates were thrown open, and the Ould Boy received Tom with bows and scrapes, and asked him his business.

"My business isn't much," replied Tom, "I have come for the loan of that flail that I see hanging on the collar-beam, for the King of Dublin to give a thrashing to the Danes."

"Well," said the other, "the Danes are much better customers to me, but since you walked so far, I won't refuse you. Hand me the flail," he said to a young imp, and he winked his far-off eye at the same time. So while some imps were barring the gates, the young devil climbed up and took down the iron flail that had the handstaff and flail both made out of red-hot iron. The little vagabond was grinning to think how it would burn the hands off Tom, but not a mark did it make on him, no more than if it was a good oak sapling.

"Thankee," said Tom, "now would you open the gates for a body and I'll give you no more trouble."

"Oh, tramp!" said Ould Nick, "Is that the way? It is easier getting inside the gates that getting out again. Take that tool from him and give him a dose of the oil of stirrup."

One fellow put out his claws to seize the flail, but Tom

gave him such a welt of it on the side of his head that he broke off one of his horns and made him roar like the devil he was. Well, they rushed at Tom, but he gave them, little and big, such a thrashing as they wouldn't forget for a while. At last said the Ould Thief to all, rubbing his elbows, "Let the fool out, and woe to whoever lets him in again, great or small."

So out marched Tom and away with him, without minding the shouting and cursing they kept up at him from the top of the walls. And when he got home to the big lawn of the palace, there never was such running and racing to see himself and the flail. When he told his story he lay the flail down on the stone steps and bid no one for their lives to touch it.

If the King, Queen, and Princess had made much of him before, they made ten times as much of him now. But Redhead, the mean scruff-hound, stole over, thinking to catch hold of the flail to make an end of him. His fingers hardly touched it when he let out a roar as if heaven and earth were coming together, and kept flinging his arms about so, and dancing about, that it was pitiful to look at him. Tom ran to him as quickly as he could, catching Redhead's hands in his own. He rubbed them this way and that and the burning pain vanished.

Well, the poor fellow, between the pain that was only just gone, and the very relief he now felt, wore the most comical face that you ever did see—it was such a *mixerum-gatherum* of laughing and crying. Everyone burst out laughing—the Princess could stop no more than the rest. And then Tom said, "Now ma'am, if there were fifty halves of you, I would hope that you'd give me them all." Well the Princess had no mock modesty about her. She looked at her father, and then went over to Tom and put her two delicate hands into his two rough ones, and every man present wished it was himself that was in Tom's shoes that day!

That evening, Tom would not bring the flail into the palace. You may be sure no other body went near it, and when early risers were passing next morning they found two long clefts in the stone where it had been before burning itself an opening downwards, nobody could tell how far. A messenger came in at noon and said that the Danes were so frightened when they heard that the flail was in Dublin that they had climbed into their ships and sailed away.

It is said that before they were married, Tom got some man like Pat Mara of Tomenine to learn him the "principles of politeness," fluxions, gunnery, fortifications, decimal fractions, practice, and the rule-of-three-direct, so that he'd be able to keep up a conversation with the royal family. Whether he ever lost his time learning those sciences, no one knows, but it's as sure as fate that his mother never more saw any want till the end of her days.

Pwyll and Rhiannon

I THE WEDDING

Nearby the castle of Narberth, occupied by Prince Pwyll and his court, was the Mound of Arberth. It was believed that whoever sat upon this Mound would have a strange adventure: either they would be struck with several blows from an invisible force or they would see a wonderful vision.

During a feast at Narberth, the Prince, full with food and drink and happy in the company of all his lords, looked over the splendid banquet scene. He had always loved these unruly events, but he found himself wanting something that would further impress his loyal men. After a few moments of thought, he decided that he would announce to all his intentions to sit on the Mound of Arberth.

So the next day, he did. While sitting on the Mound, he had a spectacular vision. A lady approached him riding on a pure white horse and wearing a golden dress. Yet when he sent his troops after her, she charged off so quickly and steadily that nobody could catch her. Then the following day, Prince Pwyll proceeded to sit on the Mound again. The beautiful woman on the white horse reappeared, but this time he did not send his troops—he went after her by himself. But she was quick and Pwyll tired quickly trying to follow her. He thought he would never catch her, so he shouted out: "O maiden, for the sake of him thou lovest most, stay for me."

"I will gladly," she replied, "but for the sake of your tired horse. It would have been better if you had asked me that earlier."

Pwyll questioned her reason for appearing to him, and she answered, "I am Rhiannon, the daughter of Hevydd Hēn, and they sought to marry me against my wishes, but I will have no husband but you. And if you reject me, I will marry no one!"

"Aie!" Pwyll replied, "if I could choose from all the women on earth, I would choose no one else but you."

The woman was flattered and they agreed that in a year's time Pwyll would come to the palace of Hevydd Hēn and claim her as his wife.

The Prince kept his agreement, he arrived at the palace with a hundred of his finest knights and found a splendid feast set out for him. He sat by his lady, and looked squarely at her father who sat directly across from them. There was great feasting and talking until suddenly a tall, noble youth, dressed in satin, walked quietly into the room, saluting all the knights as he approached Pwyll.

"Will you have a seat, young man?" Pwyll asked.

"Sorry sir, but I am a suitor," replied the noble youth, "and have come to ask something of you."

"Whatever you wish. It will please me greatly if I can provide it," Pwyll commented unknowingly.

"Ugh, you fool!" cried Rhiannon, "why did you say that?"

"Has he not asked this question of all his nobles?" the young man asked.

"Sir, it is my wish to have the bride Rhiannon, and the exact same banquet and ceremony before you now one year from today."

Pwyll was quiet.

"You can be as quiet as you like," Rhiannon said, "but never did any man make a worse use of his wits than you did just now. Do you know who that young man is? He is Gwawl, son of Clud. He was the young suitor whom I was trying to escape when I met you."

Pwyll felt bound in honor to his word and felt it necessary to comply, but it was not in his power to provide for a banquet, nor offer Rhiannon to the noble youth to wife. Thus, he was free from all demands, but Rhiannon wanted to set a trap for Gwawl. She would make herself Gwawl's bride along with a great feast in a year's time. After telling Pwyll this plan, she handed him a magical brown cloth bag, which he was to use when the time was right. A year passed, and Gwawl appeared on schedule. The feast was prepared and Gwawl sat in the seat of honor, which Pwyll had held last year. As the banquet hall roared with loud merrymaking, a beggar dressed in rags with his feet wrapped in straw walked into the hall. He was carrying a cloth bag and begged humbly for a favor from Gwawl. The beggar wished to merely fill his bag with food from the banquet table and then set off again. Gwawl gladly approved his wish, and an attendant went to fill the bag. He threw in the fruits, and then the meats, yet the bag had hardly taken on a bulge. Soon the attendant had cleared off the entire table and the goods of the banquet still had not even come close to filling the bag.

Gwawl cried out, "I can't believe this, will that bag ever be filled?"

"It will not," commented Pwyll, dressed as the beggar man, "unless some man rich in land and treasure gets into the bag and stamps down on its contents with both feet and cries, 'Enough—This bag will hold no more. I command it.'"

Rhiannon urged Gwawl to test the truth of this story. So Gwawl put both feet in to the bag and began stomping, when suddenly Pwyll quickly drew up the sides of the bag over Gwawl's head and tied a strong knot at its opening. Pwyll then blew his horn, and the knights who were hiding outside the banquet hall rushed in and captured the followers of Gwawl.

After they had bound up their enemies, the knights asked about the bag. "What's in the bag?"

"A badger," some of Pwyll's men joked.

"Well, in that case, how 'bout a game of 'Badger in the Bag?'" the others responded. Soon they had the bag bouncing against the walls and furniture as they kicked it back and forth.

After a few minutes of this, they heard a voice emit from the bag. "Sirs," yelled Gwawl, "if you hear me, listen, I do not deserve to die a wretched death in this bag!"

"He's right," said Hevydd Hēn.

They then all agreed that Gwawl should satisfy all Pwyll's knights with a feast, leave behind all hopes of ever marrying Rhiannon, and promise never to seek revenge on Pwyll. When this was confirmed by all, Gwawl and his men were freed to return to their own territory.

Prince Pwyll then wed Rhiannon and gave royal gifts to all his knights. After a splendid feast, they traveled back to the palace of Narberth in Dyfed, where Rhiannon in turn gave gifts of diamonds and precious stones to the lords and ladies of her new country. Pwyll and Rhiannon then ruled in peace for many years after their return.

II THE PENANCE

After a few years of marriage to his wife, Rhiannon, Prince Pwyll had no heir to succeed him to the throne. His advisors asked him to take another wife, and after much debate Pwyll agreed.

"Give us a year," he declared, "and if there is no heir for the throne a year from now, you'll have your wish."

Before that year had passed, a son was born to them. A total of six maids were assigned to watch over the boy, yet one night, all six maids fell asleep, and in the morning the boy was missing!

"We shall be punished severely for this," the maids exclaimed.

Out of fear for their own lives, they devised a terrible plot to escape punishment. Killing the cub of a staghound, they placed the bones by Rhiannon and smeared her face with blood as she slept. When she woke and asked for her child, they told her, "In the middle of the night, you awakened and began to devour your child. We tried to stop you, but you overpowered all of us." Rhiannon did not believe them, but there was nothing she could do.

When Pwyll heard the story, he did not imprison Rhiannon as his advisors begged him to do, but instead imposed a penance on her—she was to sit outside the south gate of the palace every day and tell the story of how she devoured her child to every stranger while carrying them on her back to the interior of the palace.

At this same time there lived a man who had the most beautiful horse in the world. His name was Teirnyon of Gwent Is Coed and his horse, though beautiful, had a peculiar misfortune. Every May the horse would give birth to a colt, but no one ever knew what became of the new-born colts as they always disappeared in the night soon after their birth. This year though, Teirnyon resolved to take the matter into his own hands, and resolved to arm himself and watch very carefully. On the night his horse gave birth to a colt, he sat up late, determined to find out what had happened. He was admiring the new colt, when suddenly, a long, clawed arm came through the door of the stable and grabbed the colt. Teirnyon lifted his sword and severed the arm at the elbow. A great roar was heard from outside the stable, and he ran to see the beast he had just smote, but he could see nothing as the dark covered everything.

When he came back to the stable, he found an infant boy wrapped in a cape of satin. He picked up the child and brought him indoors to his wife. She had no children, and was extremely happy to have the child. So glad was she about this good fortune that she told all her neighbors and friends that the child was her own. As his hair was a gold-like yellow, they named him Gwri of the Golden Hair.

The young baby grew quickly and mightily. By the time the boy was nearing two, he had the strength of a seven year old and as he was so strong, they decided to give him the colt that was born on the day they found him.

It was some time after the first year of Rhiannon's penance that Teirnyon heard about her misfortune. And as the young boy grew up, he watched him closely until he decided that this boy was indeed the son of Pwyll, Prince of Dyfed. He told his suspicions to his wife and they both decided that it would be best to take the boy to the palace and release Rhiannon from her punishment.

Teirnyon, two knights, and the boy riding his colt, approached the castle and found Rhiannon there sitting outside the south gate saying, "Good knights, go no further. I will carry each of you to the interior of the palace, if that is your wish."

But they avoided her pleas and entered the palace with Rhiannon by their side. Pwyll was glad to see Teirnyon, and brought him much food to welcome him. During their meal, Teirnyon told the story of the young boy and colt, and how they found the boy in the horse stables.

"So behold, my good Pwyll and Rhiannon, here is your son," he declared, "and whoever told you elsewise did you a great wrong."

Everyone then immediately realized that the boy was the child of Pwyll and Rhiannon and they let out a great cheer. "If this is true, then this is the end to all of my troubles," Rhiannon cried.

"Wise name for your child, your lady," a chief named Pendaran claimed, "the name Pryderi (trouble) does him right as does Pryderi, son of Pwyll, Lord of Annwn."

All complimented Pendaran for his wisdom, and they agreed that the boy should be called Pryderi. And Teirnyon went home, pleased to have his good deed rewarded with thanks and love and happiness. Pwyll offered him great gifts, but Teirnyon refused them. Pryderi was raised as a true prince, and when his father Pwyll died, he reigned in his palace over the Seven Cantrevs of Dyfed. And he added to them some other beautiful dominions, and found a women to wive named Kicva, daughter of Gwynn Gohoyw, who came of the lineage of Prince Casner of Britain.

The Three Crowns

There once was a King with three daughters. The two oldest daughters were proud and selfish, but the youngest was good and charitable. After the word got out that the King had three unwed daughters, three princes from a neighboring country came to court them. And like the King's daughters, the two eldest princes were the moral equivalent of the two eldest daughters, while the youngest prince was good and charitable like the King's youngest daughter.

One day, they were all walking down to the lake when they were approached by a poor beggar. The King refused to give him anything, and the eldest princes would not spare anything, nor would their sweethearts. But the youngest daughter and her prince gave alms to the beggar, adding some kind words to their gift.

When they all came to the lake, they found the most beautiful boat they had ever seen. The two eldest daughters and their companions were very excited about the boat and wanted to ride in it right away, but the youngest refused to get in the boat as she believed it was enchanted. The eldest sisters couldn't stand for such nonsense, so they forced the youngest daughter into the boat. Now, just after the youngest daughter entered in the boat, the King was close behind her, when a little man, only seven inches high, stood up on the deck and ordered everyone to stand back. The princes, not taking kindly to this order, went to draw their swords, but found themselves unable to do so as all their strength had left their arms. Next, the small gnome, Seven Inches, untied the boat from the dock and pushed the boat off from the dock.

Seven Inches smiled as he spoke to the King, Princes, and Princesses inside the boat, "Say goodbye to your sweethearts, proud princes! Only you, youngest prince, need not fear, as you'll see your princess again one day, and you and she will be happy for many years. Bad folks, even with all the money in the world, will never be rich." And then taking the youngest princess out of the boat, he next placed all of three sisters in another boat, and sailed off with all of them. The ladies stretched their arms towards their princes, but they couldn't say a thing.

When Seven Inches and the Princesses reached a distant shore of the lake, the three princes and the King saw Seven Inches take the women out of the boat and place them one by one into a draw-well. The men were astonished, never before had they ever seen a draw-well existing on that distant shore before. When the last princess was down the well and out of sight, the four men regained their strength in both their arms and legs and after much effort they rowed the boat back to shore. Back on land, they ran round the edge of the lake to where they found the well with a windlass that had a silk rope attached to it and a white basket attached to the rope.

"Let me go after them," said the youngest prince, "either I'll die or recover them."

"No, I'm entitled my turn before you," said the second daughter's prince.

"If anybody goes first, it's going to be me, by the right that I'm the oldest," claimed the eldest prince.

So it was decided that the eldest prince would go down the well. He hopped in the basket, and they lowered the basket until they could no longer see him. A few minutes later they felt the basket hit bottom so they stopped turning. After a few hours, they still had not heard from the eldest prince, so they went off to dinner and posted a few guards to watch over the well.

The guards remained till the next morning, when the second prince went down the well, and when he didn't come back after the second night, they sent the youngest prince down. After a long descent, he finally felt bottom. The young prince got out of the bucket and looked out at the splendid scene. There were wide green fields, dense woods, a great castle, and a brilliant blue sky overhead.

"Why, it's Tir-na-n Oge," said the prince, "I wonder who could be in that great castle over there?"

He walked across the green fields and through the dense woods till he reached the castle. There was no one there to greet him, but the large door to the castle was open.

He moved from one splendid room to another until he reached the main hall with a large oak table in the center of the room, and on top of the table was the finest dinner he had ever seen. He was hungry, but he didn't feel comfortable eating the food without being invited. So the prince sat himself down by the fire and fell asleep. He wasn't asleep for long when he heard the sound of some footsteps approaching him. It was Seven Inches and the youngest princess! The prince and princess raced into each other's arms and rejoiced in their hearts.

Seven Inches looked up at the prince and questioned him, "Why aren't you eating?"

"Well, sir," said the young prince, "I was hungry, but I think it's only right that I be asked to partake in a meal that isn't mine."

"Well," said Seven Inches, "your brothers didn't feel that to be so and look what has happened to them." The little man pointed towards two statues standing in two opposite corners of the room, which frightened the young prince considerably. Seven Inches bade the couple to sit down and enjoy themselves, which they tried to do, though his two brothers stood as stone statues nearby.

One day went by without incident, but the next day, Seven Inches came to the young prince and told him that he would have to go and find the second princess at a giant's castle that night and then find the third princess at another giant's castle the next night. "You don't need to worry about asking leave to remove the princesses as they are only housekeepers for the giants," Seven Inches exclaimed. "Maybe, if they ever get home, they'll realize that they too are just normal flesh-and-blood people like poor people."

So that day the prince left the castle to find the second princess. He reached the castle where she was staying at sunset. The princess was overwhelmed with joy to see him, but she heard the giant approach, so she hid the prince inside a closet. When the giant came in though, he sniffed the air, and then sniffed again.

"By the life of me, I smell fresh meat," said the giant.

"Well," replied the princess, "it's only the calf I killed for your meal today."

"Well, then," said he, "put it on the table, and let me have dinner!" So the giant ate the entire calf and drank a keg of wine.

But when he rose from the table, he commented, "How come I still smell fresh meat?"

"Oh," said the princess, "that's because you are tired and sleepy, so I think it best that you go off to bed."

"You're so good," says the giant, "when will you marry me? You keep putting me off."

"Don't worry, I'll marry you on St. Tibb's Eve," she said. Pleased with the answer, the giant put his arms on the table and fell asleep with his head in his dish.

The next morning after the giant had left the castle, she pointed the prince in the direction of the castle where the eldest princess was being held. When he reached his destination, practically the same things occurred as when he found the second eldest daughter, except this time, when the giant went to sleep after his meal, the prince and the eldest princess saddled two steeds in the stables and raced them out of the castle grounds. But when the horses ran down the stone path to the gate, the noise awoke the giant, who began to chase after the couple. The giant roared and shouted and cursed the couple, but the more noise he made the faster the horses ran. The prince and princess made good speed, but the giant still lurked close behind. Fortunately for the couple, the prince had not left the castle of Seven Inches without being provided with some magic objects to help him on his mission. He pulled back his steed, and threw a small, sharp knife behind his back, and up sprung a dense wood between the giant and the horses. Soon they were at the castle where the second eldest daughter was being held, and she was there on a fine horse waiting for them when they reached the front gate of the castle. But the sound of all three horses awoke the giant of the castle, and he, too, was soon chasing the prince and two princesses with all his might.

The first giant cleared the dense woods, so now both giants were on their trail. The horses were fast, but the giants were still gaining ground on them. So the prince again stopped the horses, and flung down the second knife behind him. This time, an entire field collapsed until there was a quarry a quarter of a mile deep with the bottom filled with black water. This kept the giants busy until the prince and two princesses were inside the castle of Seven Inches.

There was great rejoicing when the prince and princesses encountered the youngest princess, at least until the two eldest princesses beheld their lovers encased as stone. But while they were bemoaning the fate of the princes, Seven Inches approached the statues with a rod and turned them back into flesh and blood. Soon there was great hugging and kissing and the princes and all the princesses were paired once again. The next morning, there was a great breakfast with Seven Inches sitting at the head of the table.

After breakfast, Seven Inches took the young couples to a room where there were mounds of gold and silver and satins and silks. In the back of the room was a table with three sets of crowns. Each set contained a gold crown inside a silver crown, which itself was inside a copper crown. Seven Inches gave each of the young princesses a set of crowns with the instructions that all three couples were to be married on the same day while each one of the princesses were wearing their crowns. If the couples were to be married separately or a couple were to be married without a crown, then a terrible curse would be set against them.

So all the couples were getting ready to leave the castle and return back up the draw-well and their own land. They reached the basket, but as they were getting the eldest princess ready for the ride home, the youngest princess turned around and commented to the youngest prince, "I don't think your brothers mean any good. Keep my crowns under your cape and if you are asked to stay last, don't get into the basket, but instead, place a big stone there, and wait to see what will happen."

After the first princess was pulled up in the bucket, they pulled up the second princess and then brought the third princess. Soon it came time for the youngest prince, who was the last one left, to be pulled up. But, instead of getting in the bucket himself, he placed a few large stones in it. He then stepped aside and watched them pull up the load of stones. The bucket went up about thirty feet and came tumbling down like thunder, and the stones smashed violently against the ground below.

Well, now, the prince had nothing more to do than to walk back to the castle. There was plenty of food and drink at hand, and the castle and the grounds were so large there was much to see before he began to tire of the scene. It was less than a week when he began to lament the loss of his beloved, and after a month, he no longer knew what to do with his time.

So one morning, he walked into the treasure room and picked up a beautiful snuff box that he didn't recall seeing last time he visited the treasure room. He carefully opened the box, and out popped Seven Inches, who proceeded to walk across the table. "Prince," said Seven Inches, "I think that you are getting bored of my castle."

"If only I had my princess here," said the prince, "and saw you once and a while, I'd be happy here for a long time."

"Well," replied Seven Inches, "you've been here a good long time, and you're starting to get itchy for the world above. Here, keep this snuff box and whenever you want my help, open the box, and I'll be ready to do for you what I can." The prince thanked the little man, and then proceeded to walk through the gardens until he reached the border of the castle grounds.

Soon he found himself outside of a smith's gate that he had often passed before. It was about a mile away from the castle where his betrothed princess resided. He was walking by when the smith came out and said, "It's a shame for a strong man like yourself to be out of work when there's so much work to do. Have you ever used a hammer? If you want, come in and give me a hand. I'll be sure to pay you well, if you're a hard worker."

"Don't worry about the money," commented the prince, "all I'm seeking is employment." The smith then handed the prince a hammer, and they proceeded indoors where the smith was hammering out a set of horseshoes.

While they were hard at work, a tailor came into the room where they were working. The smith asked the tailor for any news that he might have heard recently. So the tailor replied that he heard they recovered the princesses and princes who had been missing for days with the exception of the youngest prince.

"The princesses were determined," the tailor said, "that they wouldn't marry unless all three couples were going to get married at the same time. But when they were bringing up the youngest prince, there was an accident that caused the rope to slip out the elder princes' hands. But before they heard the bucket hit bottom, the rope, the well, and windlass disappeared. There was no evidence left of their adventure at all. The elder princes were still determined to marry, so after they received the king's permission, they planned the ceremony for the next morning. The whole village was there, myself included. The brides wore splendid dresses with their sets of three crowns on their heads. Only the youngest princess was removed. She stood to the side mourning the loss of her prince. When the two bridegrooms came into the room, walking as proud as I've ever seen, they were met at the back of the hall by the King, who was leading the two bridegrooms up to the alter. Then, all of a sudden, the floorboards of the hall opened two yards wide underneath the princes, and they fell into the vaults where the dead were laid to rest. The whole place went crazed with weeping, shouting, screaming, and mass confusion. Finally, someone called the clerk who opened up the vaults from a basement door, and out stepped the two brothers, their fine clothes covered with cobwebs and dust.

"The King, realizing something of an omen in this freak accident, called off the wedding until they should find the crown of the youngest princess and marry her at the same time as the other princesses. To help speed along the matter, the King made an offer that anyone who could bring him three crowns just like the other two sets of crowns will have the opportunity to marry the young princess."

"I would like to marry her," said the smith, "but I was looking at the crowns when they were brought out and I don't think there's a smith in the world that could imitate them."

"Ah," said the prince, "a weak heart has never won a princess. Here's some money. Go to the castle and get me a quarter of a pound of gold, a quarter of a pound of silver, and a quarter of a pound of copper, and bring back the pattern of the crowns. I promise you by this time tomorrow, you shall have those things you've been asking for." The smith could hardly believe his ears, but somehow the prince had convinced him. So he went out to fetch the metals and the pattern of the crown.

When the prince received all the material he needed, he shut the doors to the forge and began fiercely hammering and pounding away. He worked the entire night, and when the sun began to rise in the East, the prince opened the doors to the forge and displayed the crowns before the crowd that had gathered there. He then gave the crowns to the smith and bid him go on his way. So the smith left his forge with the three crowns and all the town followed him to the King's castle. When the King saw the crowns he let out a great cry of joy!

"Sir," the King said to the smith, "if these crowns are

the ones, you will be a married man, my good sir."

"Aye, your majesty," the smith replied, "I didn't make these crowns at all. It was some vagabond that made them."

So the King asked his daughter if she would marry the vagabond who made these crowns. His daughter hesitated, and then asked to hold the crowns and look at them closely. When she saw the crowns she knew that her beloved prince had returned, and she gladly offered to marry the man who had made these crowns.

The King was so pleased to hear his daughter's response that he asked the eldest of the two princes to get a coach and bring the man responsible for the crowns to his castle. Now the eldest prince was not so pleased with the news, but he couldn't refuse the King's orders. When he pulled the coach up to the smith's forge and saw the vagabond there, he asked the man to get in the coach. So the young prince, disguised as a vagabond, hopped into the carriage, and while he was on his way, he opened up the snuff box, so that he could ask something of Seven Inches. "Master," replied the prince, "let me get to the forge, and let this carriage be filled with stones." No sooner had he said the words than the carriage was filled with stones.

When the carriage entered the castle yard, the King was overjoyed at the thought of meeting his new son-in-law. But when he went to open the carriage door, he was trounced by a shower of stones that soon buried him. There was great excitement and when the King got up off the ground, and wiped the blood from his forehead, he looked crossly at the eldest prince.

"Dear sire," said the eldest prince, "it wasn't my fault.

I saw the young man get into my coach and once we were on the road we didn't stop."

"Well, he did this because you were rude to him. Now," said the King to the other prince, "go back to the smith's forge, be polite, and bring the young man here."

Now when the second prince came to pick the youngest prince, he wasn't a bit kinder. So when the carriage returned to the castle, the King was covered by a great shower of mud when he went to open the carriage door.

"This is useless," said the King wiping off the mud from his face, "if I want to bring this young man here, I might as well do it myself." So after he cleaned himself from head to toe and changed his clothes, he hopped on the carriage and drove it to the smith's forge.

"Maybe my previous messengers weren't polite enough," said the King to the youngest prince, "but I would be glad to have you ride in the front of the carriage with me." But the prince begged to sit in the coach, and after much argument, he got his way. When they were about half-way to the castle, the prince opened up the snuff box, and out popped Seven Inches.

"Master," said the young prince, "I'd like to be dressed in a fashion befitting a prince."

"Well, that shall be done," says Seven Inches, "but I'm going to have to say good-bye. Be as good as you always were, and love your wife, and that's all I've got to say— so goodbye." With that, Seven Inches disappeared. Soon the carriage was brought into the castle yard, and when they opened up the door, out stepped the young prince dressed in regal splendor. Even before greeting the King, the first thing the young prince did was to race over to his bride and embrace her heartily.

There was then great joy throughout the castle yard, only the two elder princes were not so happy. All three marriages were celebrated that day, but the crowd cheered loudest when the youngest princess and youngest prince were wed, for never did they see a happier married couple. ❧

The Corpse Watchers

There was once a poor woman who had three daughters, and one day the eldest said, "Mother, bake my cake and kill my cock till I go seek my fortune." So she did, and when all was ready she asked her daughter, "Which will you have—half of these with my blessing, or the whole with my curse?"

"Curse or no curse," said the daughter, "the whole is little enough." So away she set, and if the mother didn't give her her curse, she also didn't give her her blessing.

She walked, and she walked, till she was tired and hungry, and then she sat down to take her dinner. While she was eating it a poor woman came up and asked for a bit. "The dickens a bit you'll get from me, it's all too little for myself," she snapped. The poor woman walked away looking very sorrowful. At nightfall the daughter found lodging in the home of a farmer, and the woman of the house told her that she could earn a spadeful of gold and a shovel full of silver if she would watch the corpse of her son waking in the next room. She agreed to do it and when the family went to sleep, she sat by the fire and watched over the corpse.

All at once the dead man stood up in his shroud and shouted, "All alone fair maid?" He asked this three times and when she did not answer, he turned her into a gray flag.

About a week later, the second daughter wished to go off and seek her fortune. She also left without her mother's curse or her blessing and the very same thing happened to her. She was left a gray flag standing beside the other.

Finally the youngest daughter went off in search of her two sisters and she took care to carry her mother's blessing with her.

She shared her dinner with the poor woman on the road and in gratitude the woman told her she would watch over her.

She found lodging in the same farmer's house and agreed to mind the corpse as her sisters did before her. She sat by the fire with the dog and the cat, and amused herself with some apples and nuts the farmer's wife had given her. She thought to herself what a handsome man the farmer's son had been.

At last the corpse rose and shouted, "All alone fair maid?" To which she quickly replied:

"All alone I am not,
I've little dog Doues, and Pussy, my cat;
I've apples to roast and nuts to crack,
And all alone I am not."

"Ho, ho!" he said, "you're a girl of courage, though you wouldn't have enough to follow me. I am now going to cross the Quaking Bog, and go through the Burning Forest. I must then enter the Cave of Terror and climb the Hill of Glass, and drop from the top of it into the Dead Sea."

"I'll follow you," she said, "for I'm engaged to mind you."

He tried to prevent her, but she was determined. He jumped through the window and she followed him until they came to the Green Hills.

"Open, open, Green Hills, and let the light of the Green Hills through," he said.

"Aye," said the girl, "and let the fair maid too."

They opened and the man and the woman passed through and found themselves standing on the edge of the Bog.

He carefully walked over shaky bits of moss and sod. While she was thinking how she could get across, the old beggar woman appeared to her and touched her shoes with a stick. Her soles spread a foot on each side and she easily got over the shaky marsh. The Burning Forest was at the edge of the Bog, and there the good fairy flung a damp, thick cloak over her so she could pass through the flames, and not a hair on her head was singed. Then they traveled through the dark Cavern of Terrors where she would have heard the most horrible yells, were it not for the good fairy stopping her ears with wax.

When they got out of the cave they were at the Mountain of Glass, and then with a tap of her rod, the good fairy made her slippers so sticky that she followed the young corpse quite easily to the top. The Dead Sea was a quarter of a mile under them, and so the corpse said to her, "Go home to my mother and tell her how far you came to do her bidding. Farewell!" He sprang head-first into the sea and she plunged in after him without even stopping to think about it.

She was stupefied at first, but when they reached the waters she recovered her thoughts. After piercing down a great depth, they saw a green light towards the bottom. At last they were below the sea and seated in a beautiful meadow. She was half asleep, her head resting against his side. When she woke, she was in bed at his house, and he and his mother were sitting and watching her.

It was a witch that had placed a curse on the young man because he would not marry her. She kept him in a state between life and death till a young woman would rescue him by doing what the girl had done. So, at her request, her sisters got their own shapes again, and were sent back to their mother with their spades of gold and shovels of silver. The youngest got the young gentleman for her husband and they lived together happily. ❧

Tain Bo Cuailgne

(The Cattle Raid of Quelgny)

There once was a wealthy Ulster farmer named Crundchu, son of Agnoman, and he dwelt in a solitary place among the hills. Now Crundchu found one day in his *dūn* a young woman of great beauty and in splendid array, whom he had never seen before. He was a widower, his wife having died after bearing him four sons, and so the strange woman, without a word, set herself to do the household tasks, prepared dinner, milked the cow, and took on herself all the duties of the mistress of the household. At night she lay down at Crundchu's side, and thereafter dwelt with him as his wife, and they loved each other dearly. Her name was Macha.

One day Crundchu was readying himself to go to a great

fair, where there would be feasting and horse racing, tournaments and music, and merrymaking of all kinds for the men of Ulster. Macha begged her husband not to go, but he persisted.

"Then," she pleaded, "at least do not speak of me, for I may dwell with you only so long as I am not spoken of."

Crundchu promised to obey her injunction, and off he went to the fair, where the King's two horses carried off prize after prize in the races.

"I have a wife at home," said Crundchu, in a moment of forgetfulness, "who can run quicker than these horses.

"Seize that man," cried the King, "and hold him until his wife is brought to the contest."

So the King's messengers fetched Macha, who was with child, and brought her before the assembly. When the King bade her prepare for the race, she pleaded her condition, saying, "I am close upon my hour."

"Then hew her man in pieces," said the King to his guards.

Macha turned to the bystanders, crying "Help me, for a mother has borne each of you! Give me but a short delay until I am delivered."

But the King and all the crowd in their savage lust for sport would hear of no delay.

"Then bring up the horses," said Macha, "and because you have no pity a heavier infamy shall fall upon you."

So she raced against the horses, and outran them, but as she came to the goal she let forth a great cry and gave birth to twins. As she uttered that cry, however, all the spectators felt themselves seized with pangs like her own, and they, too, had no more strength than a woman in her time.

And so it was prophesied by Macha that from this hour the shame they had wrought on her would fall upon each man of Ulster, and in the hours of their greatest need they would be as weak and helpless as women in childbirth, and this would endure for five days and four nights, and the curse should be to the ninth generation. And so it came to pass, and this is the cause of the debility of the Ultonians that was wont to afflict the warriors of the province.

Now in the land of Rathcroghan, Ailell was King, but Queen Maev was the ruler in truth, and ordered all things as she wished, and took what husbands she wished, and dismissed them at pleasure. She was as fierce and strong as a goddess of war, and knew no law but her own wild will. And so it was that when a young Prince named Fergus mac Roy came to her in her palace in Roscommon she gave him her love, as she had given it to many before, and they plotted together how to attack and devastate the Province of Ulster.

It so happened that Maev possessed a famous red bull with a white front and horns named Finnbenach, and one day when she and Ailell were counting up their respective possessions, he had taunted her because the Finnbenach would not stay in the hands of a woman, but had attached himself to Ailell's herd. Maev, much vexed, went to her steward, mac Roth, and asked him if there was anywhere in Erin a bull as fine as the Finnbenach.

"Truly," said the steward, "there is—for the Brown Bull of Quelgny, that belongs to Dara, son of Fachtna, is the mightiest beast in Ireland."

And after that Maev felt as if she had no flocks and herds worth anything at all unless she could possess the

Brown Bull of Quelgny. But the Brown Bull was in Ulster, and the Ulstermen knew the treasure they possessed, and Maev knew that they would not give up the Bull without fighting for it. So she and Fergus and Ailell agreed to make a foray against Ulster for the Brown Bull, and thus to go to war with the province, for Fergus longed to avenge an old wrong, and Maev for fighting, glory, and the Bull, and Ailell to satisfy Maev.

Maev first sent an embassy to Dara, offering recompense of fifty heifers, and many other treasures, for the loan of the bull for a year. But Dara, in the beginning delighted by the prospect, soon heard tales about Maev's messengers, and how they said that if the bull was not yielded willingly it would be taken by force, and so he sent back a message of refusal and defiance.

"'Twas known," said Maev, "the bull will not be yielded by fair means, he shall now be won by foul."

And so Maev sent messengers around on every side to summon her armies for the raid. Then there came all the mighty men of Connacht—first the seven Mainés, sons of Ailell and Maev, each with his retinue, and Ket and Anluan, sons of Maga, with thirty hundreds of armed men, and yellow-haired Ferdia, with his company of Firbolgs, boisterous giants who delighted in war and in strong ale. And there came also the allies of Maev—an army of the men of Leinster, who so excelled in warlike skills that they were broken up and distributed among the companies of Connacht, lest they should prove a danger to the army, and Cormac, son of Conor, with Fergis mac Roy and other exiles from Ulster, who had revolted against Conor for his treachery to the Sons of Usna.

But before the army set forth, Maev sent her spies into

Ulster to learn of their battle preparations. When the spies returned they brought back a wondrous tale that rejoiced the heart of Maev— Conor, the King, lay in pangs at Emain Macha, while his son Cuscrid in his island-fortress and Owen Prince of Ferney were helpless as children. Celtchar, the huge gray warrior, son of Ulthecar Hornskin, and even Conall of the Victories, lay moaning and writhing on their beds, and there was no hand in Ulster that could lift a spear.

After hearing the spies' story Maev quickly went to her chief Druid to learn what her own lot in war should be.

But the Druid only said, "Whoever comes back in safety, or comes not, you yourself shall return."

Maev departed, puzzled by her Druid's remarks. As she continued riding she saw suddenly standing before her chariot-pole a young maiden with tresses of yellow hair that fell below her knees, clad in a mantle of green, and with a shuttle of gold she was weaving a fabric upon a loom.

"Who are you, girl?" asked Maev, "And what are you doing?"

"I am the prophetess Fedelma, from the Fairy Mound of Croghan," said the maid, "and I weave the four provinces of Ireland together for the foray into Ulster."

"What do you see for our army?" asked Maev.

"I see them all be-crimsoned red," replied the prophetess.

"Yet all the Ulster heroes are in their pangs—there is none that can lift a spear against us," said Maev.

"I see the army all be-crimsoned," said Fedelma, "I see a man of small stature, but the hero's light is on his brow— a young and modest lad, but in battle a dragon; he is

Cuchulain of Murthemney. For the son of the god Lugh is not subject to the curse of Macha, he does wondrous feats with his weapons, and by him your armies shall be slain thickly."

After speaking these words, the weaving maiden vanished, and Maev drove homewards to Rathcroghan wondering at what she had seen and heard.

The next day the armies set forth with Fergus mac Roy leading them. As they neared the confines of Ulster he bade them keep sharp watch lest Cuchulain of Murthemney, who guarded the passes of Ulster to the south, should fall upon them unawares. Now Cuchulain and his mortal father, Sualtam, were on the borders of the province, and Cuchulain, from a warning Fergus had sent him, suspected the approach of a great army. He bade Sualtam to go northwards to Emania and warn the men of Ulster.

Cuchulain then followed hard on Maev's army. As he went he estimated by the tracks they had left that the number of the army was 54,000. Circling around the army, he met them in front, and soon came upon two chariots containing scouts sent ahead by Maev. These he slew, each man with his driver, and having with one sweep of his sword cut a forked pole deep into a river-ford at the place called Athgowla, impaled on each prong a bloody head. When the army came up they wondered and feared at the sight, and Fergus declared that they were under a spell not to pass that ford until one of them had plucked out the pole even as it was driven in, with the fingertips of one hand. So Fergus dove into the water to attempt the feat, and seventeen chariots were broken under him as he tugged at the pole, but at last he tore it out. As it was now late, the army encamped upon the spot. These devices of Cuchulain were intended to delay the invaders until the Ulster men had recovered from their debility.

When the army proceeded on its way the next day, Cuchulain heard the noise of timber being cut. Going into the woods he found a charioteer belonging to a son of Ailell and Maev cutting down chariot-poles of holly.

"What are you doing, sir?" he asked the charioteer.

"I am fixing the chariots that were damaged while we chased Cuchulain, the Hound of Ulster."

The driver did not recognize his companion, since at ordinary times Cuchulain appeared as a slight and unimposing figure and only in battle did he dilate in size and undergo a fearful distortion.

"I wish to help you with the chariots. Shall I cut the poles or trim them?"

"You may do the trimming," said the driver.

Cuchulain then took the poles by the tops and drew them against the set of the branches between his toes and ran his fingers down them the same way giving them over as smooth and polished as if they were planed by a carpenter.

The driver stared at him and asked in fear and amazement, "I doubt this work I asked you to do is your proper work. Who are you?"

"I am that Cuchulain of whom you spoke earlier."

"Surely I am but a dead man!" cried the driver.

"Nay," replied Cuchulain, "I slay not drivers nor messengers nor men unarmed. But run and tell your master Orlam that Cuchulain is about to visit him."

The driver immediately ran off, but Cuchulain outstripped him and met Orlam first, striking off his head.

He then shook this trophy before the army of Maev, allowing them their first glimpse of their persecutor.

After this atrocity, the army of Maev spread out and devastated the territories of Bregia and of Murthemney. However, they could not advance further into Ulster, for Cuchulain hovered about them continually, slaying them by twos and threes, and no man knew where he would swoop next. As Cuchulain's wrath grew fiercer, he descended with supernatural might upon whole companies of the Connacht army and hundreds fell at his onset. He became a fearsome and multiform creature as never was known before. Every particle of him quivered like a bulrush in a running stream. His calves and heels and hams shifted to the front, and his feet and knees turned to the back, and the muscles of his neck stood out like the head of a young child. One eye was engulfed deep in his head, the other protruded, his mouth met his ears, and foam poured from his jaws like the fleece of a three-year-old ram. The beats of his heart sounded like the roars of a lion as he rushed on his prey. A light blazed upon his head, and his hair became tangled about as if it had been the branches of a red thorn bush tuffed into the gap of a fence. Taller, thicker, more rigid, longer than the mast of a great ship was the perpendicular jet of dusky blood which out of his scalp's very central point shot upwards and was there scattered to the four cardinal points, whereby was formed a magic mist of gloom resembling the smoky pall that drapes a regal dwelling, what time a king at nightfall of a winter's day draws near to it. At the sight of Cuchulain in his paroxysm a hundred of Maev's warriors fell dead from horror.

"I will try to persuade him to desert the cause of Ulster

and join us," said Maev, who was greatly awed and impressed by Cuchulain's fury.

So she arranged for a meeting with him and tried to tempt him with promises of glory. As she met with him, she scanned him closely and was struck by his slight and boyish appearance.

Cuchulain was greatly insulted by her offer and said, "You fail to move me from my loyalty to Ulster and death will now descend even more thickly than ever upon the Connacht army." The promise was not an idle one and was soon carried out.

The men became afraid to move out for plunder save in twenties and thirties. At night the stones from Cuchulain's sling whistled continually through the camp, braining or maiming. At last through the mediation of Fergus, an agreement was arranged.

"I will not harry the army provided that they send against me only one champion at a time, whom I will meet in battle at the ford of the River Dee. While each fight is in progress the army might move on, but when it is ended they must encamp until the next morning," ordered Cuchulain.

"Tis better to lose one man a day than a hundred," said Maev, as the pact was made.

As Cuchulain fought the single combats he was always the victor. Maev tried to persuade Fergus to challenge Cuchulain, but neither Fergus nor Cuchulain would agree to fight each other. Instead they made a bargain where Cuchulain would pretend to attack Fergus when necessary as long as Fergus would do the same for him.

During one of Cuchulain's duels Maev, with a third of her army, made a sudden foray into Ulster and penetrated as far as Dunseverick, on the northern coast, plundering and ravaging as they went. The raiders of Maev found the Brown Bull there and drove him off with the herd in triumph, passing Cuchulain as they returned. Cuchulain rushed after them and slew the leader of the escort but he could not rescue the Bull.

The raid ought now to have ended, for its object had been obtained, but by this time the armies of the four southern provinces had gathered together under Maev for the plunder of Ulster, and Cuchulain remained still the solitary warder of the marches. Nor did Maev keep her agreement, for bands of twenty warriors at a time were loosed against him and he had much to do to defend himself.

The next champion sent against him by Maev was Loch, son of Mofebis. To meet this hero Cuchulain had to stain his chin with blackberry juice so as to simulate a beard, lest Loch should disdain to do combat with a boy. So they fought at the ford, and a fierce battle ensued until Cuchulain finally drove the *Gae Bolg* against Loch, splitting his heart in two.

"Suffer me to rise," said Loch, "that I may fall on my face on your side of the ford, and not backward toward the men of Erin."

"'Tis a warrior's boon you ask for," said Cuchulain, "and it is granted."

When Loch died a great despondency fell upon Cuchulain, for he was wearied with continued fighting, and sorely wounded, and he had never slept since the beginning of the raid, save leaning upon his spear. He then decided to send his charioteer, Laeg, to see if he could rouse the men of Ulster to come to his aid at last. But still the men of Ulster lay helpless.

Next the men of Erin resolved to send against Cuchulain, in single combat, the Clan Calatin. Now Calatin was a wizard, and he and his twenty-seven sons formed, as it were, but one being, the sons being organs of their father, and what any one of them did they all did alike. They were all poisonous, so that any weapon which one of them used would kill in nine days the man who was but grazed by it. When this multiform creature met Cuchulain each hand of it hurled a spear at once, but Cuchulain caught the twenty-eight spears on his shield and not one of them drew blood. Then he drew his sword to lop off the spears that bristled from his shield, but as he did so the Clan Calatin rushed upon him and flung him down, thrusting his face into the gravel. At this Cuchulain gave a great cry of distress at the unequal combat, and one of the Ulster exiles, Fiach, son of Firaba, who was with the army of Maev, and was looking on at the fight, could not endure to see the plight of the champion, so he drew his sword and with one stroke lopped off the twenty-eight hands that were grinding the face of Cuchulain into the gravel of the ford. Then Cuchulain arose and hacked the Clan Calatin into fragments, so that none survived to tell Maev what Fiacha had done.

Cuchulain had now overcome all the mightiest of Maev's men, save only the mightiest of them all after Fergus—Ferdia, son of Daman.

Maev went to him and bade him, "You are a great champion equal to Cuchulain. You must be the next to do battle with him."

"I cannot since I am an old friend and fellow pupil of Cuchulain. I will never go out against him," he answered.

"Even as I am begging you you will not go?" she asked.

"I cannot and I will not."

At last in her anger she said, "If you do not go the poets and satirists of Erin will make verses on you and put you to open shame."

In wrath and sorrow he consented to go and told his charioteer to make ready for tomorrow's fray. Then was gloom among all his people when they heard of that, for they knew that if Cuchulain and their master met, one of them would return alive no more.

Very early in the morning Ferdia drove to the ford and lay down there on the cushions and skins of the chariot and slept until Cuchulain should come. Not until it was full daylight did Ferdia's charioteer hear the thunder of Cuchulain's war-car approaching, and then he woke his master. The two friends faced each other across the ford.

And when they had greeted each other Cuchulain said, "It is not you, O Ferdia, who should have come to do battle with me. When we were with Skatha did we not go side by side in every battle, through every wood and wilderness? Were we not heart-companions, comrades, in the feast and the assembly? Did we not share one bed and one deep slumber?"

But Ferdia replied, "O Cuchulain, you of the wondrous feats, though we have studied poetry and science together, and though I have heard you recite our deeds of friendship, yet it is my hand that shall wound you. I bid you remember not our comradeship, O Hound of Ulster. It shall not avail you, it shall not avail you."

For three days they did battle with each other. On the fourth day Ferdia knew the contest would be decided, and he armed himself with special care. As he waited by the ford he tossed up his weapons and caught them again and did many wonderful feats, playing with his mighty weapons as a juggler plays with apples.

And Cuchulain, watching him, said to Laeg, his driver, "If I give ground today, you must reproach and mock me and spur me on to valor, and praise and hearten me if I do well, for I shall have need of all my courage."

"O Ferdia," said Cuchulain, when they met, "what shall be our weapons today?"

"It is your choice today," said Ferdia.

"Then let it be all or none," said Cuchulain.

And Ferdia was downcast at hearing this, but he said, "So be it."

Till midday they fought with spears and none could gain any advantage over the other. Then Cuchulain drew his sword and sought to smite Ferdia over the rim of his shield, but Ferdia's giant horse, Firbolg, flung him off. Thrice Cuchulain leaped high into the air, seeking to strike Ferdia over his shield, but each time as he descended Ferdia caught him upon the shield and flung him off like a little child into the ford.

Laeg continually mocked him, crying, "He casts you off as a river flings its foam, he grinds you as a millstone grinds a corn of wheat. You are an elf, never call yourself a warrior!"

Then at last Cuchulain's frenzy came upon him, and he dilated giant-like, until he overtopped Ferdia, and the hero-light blazed about his head. In close contact the two were interlocked, whirling and trampling, while the demons and goblins and unearthly things of the glens screamed from the edges of their swords, and the waters of the ford recoiled in terror from them, so that for a while they fought on dry land in the midst of the riverbed. And now Ferdia found Cuchulain a moment off his guard and smote him with the edge of the sword, and it sank deep into his flesh, and all the river ran red with his blood. He pressed Cuchulain sorely after that, hewing and thrusting so that Cuchulain could endure it no longer, and he shouted to Laeg to fling him the *Gae Bolg*. Cuchulain seized the *Gae Bolg* in his toes and drove it upward against Ferdia, and it pierced through the iron apron and burst in three the millstone that guarded him, and deep into his body it passed, so that every crevice and cranny of him was filled with its barbs.

"Tis enough!" cried Ferdia, "I have my death of that. It is an ill deed that I fall by your hand, O Cuchulain."

Cuchulain seized him as he fell and carried him northward across the ford so that he might die on the further side of it and not on the side of the men of Erin. As he laid him down, a faintness seized Cuchulain, and he fell.

Laeg cried, "Rise up, Cuchulain, for the army of Erin will be upon us. No single combat will they give after Ferdia has fallen!"

But Cuchulain said, "Why should I rise again, O my servant, now he that lies here has fallen by my hand?"

Cuchulain then fell in a swoon-like death. And the army of Maev with tumult and rejoicing, with tossing of spears and shouting of war-songs, poured across the border into Ulster. But before they left the ford they took the body of Ferdia and laid it in a grave. They built a mound over him and set up a pillar-stone with his name and lineage.

And from Ulster came certain friends of Cuchulain who bore him away into Murthemney, where they washed him and bathed his wounds in the streams. His kin among the Danaan folk cast magical herbs into the rivers for his healing. But he lay there in weakness and in a stupor for many days.

Now Sualtam, the mortal father of Cuchulain, had taken his son's horse, the Gray of Macha, and ridden off again to see if he might rouse the men of Ulster to defend the province.

He went crying abroad, "The men of Ulster are being slain, the women carried captive, the cows driven!"

Yet they stared at him stupidly, as though they knew not of what he spoke. At last he came to Emania and there were Cathbad the Druid and Conor the King and all their nobles and lords.

Sualtam cried aloud to them, "The men of Ulster are being slain, the women carried captive, the cows driven, and Cuchulain alone holds the gap of Ulster against the four provinces of Erin. Arise and defend yourselves!"

But Cathbad only said, "Death is the reward of those who disturb the King."

"Yet it is true what the man says," replied Conor.

And the lords of Ulster wagged their heads and murmured, "True indeed it is."

Then Sualtam wheeled around his horse in anger and was about to depart when, with a start which the Gray made, his neck fell against the sharp rim of the shield upon his back which tore off his head. Yet even as the head fell on the ground it went on crying its message.

At last Conor ordered, "Put the head on a pillar so that it might be at rest."

But it still went on crying and exhorting until it finally penetrated the King's clouded mind with the truth. Soon the glazed eyes of the warriors began to glow and slowly the spell of Macha's curse was lifted from their minds and bodies.

Then Conor, arising and swearing a mighty oath, said, "The heavens are above us and the earth beneath us, and the sea is around about us; and surely, unless the heavens fall on us and the earth opens to swallow us up, and the sea overwhelms the earth, I will restore every woman to her hearth and every cow to its bier."

His Druid proclaimed, "The hour is propitious."

"Messengers, go forth to every part of the countryside and summon Ulster to arms!" ordered the King.

With the curse now departed from them the men of Ulster flocked joyfully to the summons. On every hand there was grinding of spears and swords and buckling on of armor and harnessing of war-chariots. One army came under Conor the King and Keltchar, son of Uthecar Hornskin, from Emania southwards and another from the west along the very track of the host of Maev. And Conor's army fell upon eight score of the men of Erin in Meath, who were carrying away a great booty of women-captives. Conor's army slew every man of the eight score and rescued the women.

Maev and her army then fell back toward Connacht, but when they reached the Hill of Slane, in Meath, the Ulster bands joined each other there and prepared to give battle. Maev sent her messenger mac Roth to view the Ulster army on the Plain of Garach and report upon it.

Mac Roth returned with an awe-striking description of what he beheld, "When I first looked I saw the plain covered with deer and other wild beasts."

"These," explained Fergus, "had been driven out of the forests by the advancing army of the Ulster men."

"The second time I looked I saw a mist that filled the

valleys, the hill-tops standing above it like islands. Out of the mist there came thunder and flashes of light and a wind that nearly threw me off my feet!"

"What is this?" asked Maev.

"The mist is the deep breathing of the warriors as they march, and the thunder is the clanging of their war-cars and the clash of their weapons as they go to fight," answered Fergus.

"We have warriors to meet them," said Maev confidently.

"You will need that," sighed Fergus, "for in all Ireland, nay, in all the Western world, to Greece and Scythia and the Tower of Bregon and the Island of Gades, there lives no person who can face the men of Ulster in their wrath."

The battle soon continued on the Plain of Garach, in Meath. Fergus, wielding a two-handed sword, made circles like the arch of a rainbow sweeping down whole ranks of the Ulster men at each blow, while the fierce Maev charged three times into the heart of the enemy.

Cuchulain in his stupor heard the crash of Fergus's blows.

"What is that noise?" asked Cuchulain, as he struggled to wake himself.

"It is the sword-play of Fergus," said Laeg.

Upon hearing this, Cuchulain sprang up, and his body dilated so that the wrappings and swathings that had been bound on him flew off. Arming himself he rushed into battle to meet with Fergus.

"Turn hither, Fergus!" he shouted, "I will wash you as foam in a pool, I will go over you as the tail goes over a cat, I will strike you as a mother strikes her infant."

"Who speaks to me in this way?" cried Fergus.

"Cuchulain mac Sualtam! And now you must avoid me as you have pledged earlier."

"I have promised even that," said Fergus resignedly.

And on that note Fergus exited the battle along with the men of Leinster and the men of Munster, leaving Maev with her seven sons and the army of Connacht alone.

It was midday when Cuchulain entered the fight. By evening the army of Connacht was in full flight towards the border. And Ailell and Maev made peace with Ulster for seven years, and the Ulster men returned to Emain Macha with great glory.

As for the Brown Bull of Quelgny that had been the cause of the invasion into Ulster, it met the white-horned Bull of Ailell on the Plain of Aei. The two beasts fought and the Brown Bull quickly slew the other and tossed his fragments about the land so that pieces of him were strewn from Rathcroghan to Tara. The Bull then careened madly about until he fell dead, bellowing and vomiting black gore, at the Ridge of the Bull, between Ulster and Iveagh.

Thus ends the tale. ⁊

The Voyage
of Maeldūn

Τhere once was a famous member of the Owen clan
of Aran named Ailill Edge-of-Battle, and he was known
far and wide as a masterful warrior who never lost a fight.
Now when Ailill went off with the King of Aran on a raid
of a nearby territory they made their camp near a convent one night. At midnight, Ailill was out for a walk when
he saw a nun come out of the convent to ring the bell for
midnight prayers. Ailill, though a brave warrior, was neither a kind nor well-intentioned man, so he grabbed the
nun and had his way with her. When he left in the morning she said to him only, "What is your name and where
do you come from?"

"My name is Ailill Edge-of Battle, of the Owen clan,

and I am from Aran," so saying, he took his leave from her.

It was on a hazy day a fortnight later that Ailill Edge-of-Battle was slain. He was seeking refuge in a church in Doocloone when his enemies, scavenging thieves from Leix, having heard that Ailill Edge-of Battle was inside, set the church on fire. Ailill's body was buried in the rubble and remained there for many years, as the church was never rebuilt.

In due time a son was born to the nun and she named him Maeldūn. She took him secretly to her friend, the Queen of the territory who was kind, and she raised Maeldūn as her own son.

Maeldūn grew to be a beautiful boy. His mirth was limitless, his guile incalculable. He learned to be a great warrior, and the Queen would often say to herself, "He shows his father's likeness."

One day a brash young warrior whom Maeldūn had bested taunted him with his parentage. "How can such a great warrior have no father?" the warrior said and Maeldūn gave him a sound thrashing. However, beating the young warrior did not help. Maeldūn could not beat the truth—he did not know his father. So he went to his foster-mother, the Queen.

"I will not eat, drink, or sleep until you tell me of my mother and father."

"I am thy mother," the Queen replied. "For surely no woman ever loved her son more than I love you."

However, Maeldūn would not be swayed, and he insisted on knowing everything about his parents. So the Queen finally told him of his nun-mother. The next morning he set out for her convent.

When he arrived he knew immediately which nun was his mother and she knew at once that this warrior-boy was her son. He asked her of his father and she told him only, "Your father was Ailill of the Owen clan of Aran."

Now Ailill Edge-of-Battle was still a respected man long after his death. So Maeldūn set off to Aran to meet his family and to claim his place as son of a great warrior. He took with him his three foster brothers, sons of the King and Queen who had reared him, and when he arrived in Aran he was well received.

After a while in Aran, Maeldūn happened to be with a group of young warriors who were throwing stones for sport. It so happened that the stones came from the ruins of the church of Doocloone. Maeldūn was about to take his turn throwing when a monk by the name of Briccne came to him and said, "It would be better for you to avenge the man buried beneath your feet than to uncover his bones."

"What man is buried here?" asked Maeldūn.

"Tis none other than your father, Ailill," replied the monk.

"How came my father to be buried beneath a burnt church?" Maeldūn demanded.

"Brigands from Leix burnt it to the ground while he was inside."

Maeldūn threw down the stone he was about to cast, put his cloak around his shoulders, and went home. When he asked the way to Leix, he was told he could go there only by sea. So he then went to seek the advice of a Druid on what needed to be done to get to Leix.

The wizard told him, "When you build the boat for this voyage it must be built of skins lapped threefold one over the other and only seventeen men must accompany you—not more, not less. You must begin working on the boat on the day that the sun rises highest in the East, and you must put out to sea on the longest day of the year."

Maeldūn thanked him for his help and was ready to part when the Druid grabbed his arm and whispered in a strangled voice, "Remember if you betray the oracle in any way you will be punished for the transgression."

"Fear not," he replied, "I will be faithful to you and the oracle."

Maeldūn followed the instructions carefully, and the day finally came when he and his company were ready to set out to sea. He had but hoisted the sail and gone a little way when he saw his foster-brothers come running down the beach.

"Brother, we beg of you to take us with you! We want to help you avenge the wrong done to you and your father!" they cried.

"You can only assist me by going home," said Maeldūn, "for none but the number I have may go with me."

But as he said these words the three youths flung themselves into the sea and would surely have drowned if Maeldūn had not forced the ship to turn back. As his crew fished the men out of the waters and onto the boat, Diuran the Rhymer, a fellow warrior and a God-fearing man warned, "We shall surely suffer for not heeding the warnings of the Druid."

Maeldūn and his men, now numbering twenty, rowed all day and half the night until they reached two small bare islands with only two forts visible. As they neared the islands they overheard the sound of a heated battle ensuing. Great billows of smoke and hundreds of armored men swarmed around the forts in mass confusion. However, the voice of a single soldier was heard above the din and the clamor.

"Stand off from me," he ordered, "for I am a better man than thou. 'Twas I who slew Ailill Edge-of-Battle and burned the church of Doocloone over him. No kinsman has avenged his death on me, and *thou* hast never done the like of that!"

When Maeldūn heard this boast he shouted the command to land, and his men said that God must have guided them to this spot where the slayer dwelled. However, just as they were about to anchor, a strange wind suddenly arose and blew them off into the boundless ocean.

Maeldūn, greatly angered and frustrated by being denied his vengeance, turned on his foster-brothers and said in fury, "You have caused this to be! You cast yourselves on board in spite of the words of the Druid! Now, we are all to suffer for your impudence and disrespect!" The three had no answer, save only to be silent.

The ship then drifted three days and three nights, and the men did not know whether to row or not. Then on the third day they heard the noise of breakers and came to an island as soon as the sun was up. Being hungry, they tried to land to search for food. But before they could put to shore, they met a swarm of ferocious ants, each the size of a foal, which came down and into the sea to get at them. The men made off quickly from the Island of the Ants and saw no land for three days more.

The next land they encountered was the Island of the Giant Horses. But before they attempted to put to shore Maeldūn, recalling their previous experience, said, "Let us all draw lots to decide who will be the first to explore the area. We must make sure that we shall not encounter any more beasts."

So they all drew lots and it fell to Diuran and another warrior named Germān. When they searched the island they found a vast green racecourse, on which were the marks of horses' hoofs, each as big as the sail of a ship. Nutshells of monstrous size were also lying about, along with much plunder.

Diuran and Germān, frightened by what they saw, ran back to the ship hastily and cried, "We've come upon an assembly of demons! Set sail, set sail!"

From the sea they saw a horserace in progress and heard the shouting of a great multitude. The giant horses were running swifter than the wind. So the men rowed away with all their might while crossing themselves and offering prayers.

A full week passed until they arrived at the Island of the Apples. By this time they had been a long time voyaging, food had failed them, and they were hungry. The island had precipitous sides from which a wood hung down where many apples were flourishing.

"As we pass along the cliffs," said Maeldūn, "I will hold out this twig I have broken off from the branch of that tree while we try to find somewhere to land."

For three days and nights they coasted the cliff and found no entrance to the island, but by that time a cluster of three apples had grown on the end of Maeldūn's rod, and each apple would suffice the crew for forty days.

They then came upon the Island of the Biting Horses. Here were many great beasts resembling horses, that continually tore pieces of flesh from each other's sides, so that all the island ran with blood. The men rowed hastily away, and were now disheartened and full of complaints, for they knew not where they were, nor how to find guidance or aid in their quest.

By the time they arrived at the Island of the Little Cat they had finished their supply of apples. They landed so hungry and thirsty that all the men went out to explore together. They soon found a tall white tower of chalk reaching up to the clouds, and on the rampart about it were great houses white as snow. They entered the largest of them and found no man in it but a small cat playing on four stone pillars which were in the midst of the house, leaping from one to the other. The cat looked a little on the Irish warriors, but did not cease from its play.

On the walls of the house there were three rows of objects hanging up, one row of brooches of gold and silver, and one of neck-torques of gold and silver, each as big as the hoop of a cask, and one of great swords with gold and silver hilts. Quilts and shining garments lay in the room, and there, also, was a roasted ox, a flitch of bacon, and an abundance of liquor.

"Has this been left for us?" inquired Maeldūn to the cat.

It looked at him a moment, and then continued its play.

Maeldūn turned to his men and said, "Let us eat, drink, and sleep and then store up what remainder of food we have left over. This cat is apparently our host for the evening and we, as his guests, should respect him as such."

So there they stayed and had an enjoyable meal while their host leapt from pillar to pillar. The next day, as they made ready to leave the house, the youngest of Maeldūn's foster-brothers took a necklace from the wall and was bearing it out when the cat suddenly leaped through him like a fiery arrow and he fell, a heap of ashes, on the floor. Thereupon Maeldūn, who had forbidden the theft of any of the jewels, soothed the cat and replaced the necklace. They then strewed the ashes of the dead youth on the sea-shore and put to sea again.

In the midst of Maeldūn's lamentation, the ship suddenly came upon the Island of the Black Mourners where there were many black people continually weeping and sobbing. One of the two remaining foster-brothers set foot to land and immediately became black, and fell to weeping like the rest. The two other men who went to fetch him had the same fate befall them.

Maeldūn, startled at the transformations, instructed four of his crew, "Go to the island with your heads wrapped in cloth so that you may not look on the land or breathe in the air of the place."

They seized two of the lost ones and brought them away, but were unable to reach the foster-brother. The two rescued men could not explain their conduct except by saying that they had to do as they saw others doing about them. Rather than risk losing any more men to the Island of the Black Mourners they decided to head back out to the sea.

After sailing for countless days they reached a land that had on it a fortress with a brazen door and a bridge of glass leading to it. When they sought to cross the bridge it threw them backward. A woman came out of the fortress with a pail in her hand and lifted from the bridge a slab of glass. She then let down her pail into the water beneath and returned to the fortress. They struck on the brazen portcullis before them to gain admittance, but the melody given forth by the metal plunged them in slumber until the next morning. Three times this happened, with the woman each time making an ironical speech about Maeldūn. On the fourth day, however, she came out to them over the bridge wearing a white mantle with a circlet of gold on her hair, two silver sandals on her rosy feet, and a silken smock next to her skin.

"My welcome to thee, O Maeldūn," she said and she greeted each man of the crew by his own name.

Then she took them into the great house and allotted a couch to the chief and one for each three of his men. She gave them abundance of food and drink, all out of her one pail, and each man found in it what he most desired. When she had departed they asked Maeldūn if they should woo the maiden for him.

"How would it hurt you to speak with her?" said Maeldūn cryptically.

They did so and she replied, "I know not, nor have ever known, what sin is." Twice over this is repeated. "Tomorrow," she said at last, "you shall have your answer."

When the morning came, however, they found themselves once more at sea, with no sign of the island or fortress or lady.

They then traveled for many days and many nights until they came to a great silvern column, four-square, rising from the sea. Each of its four sides was as wide as two oar-strokes of the boat. Not a sod of earth was at its foot, but it rose from the boundless ocean and its summit was lost in the sky. From that summit a huge silver net was flung far away into the sea and through a mesh of that net they sailed. As they did so Diuran hacked away a piece of the net.

"Destroy it not," said Maeldūn, "for what we see is the work of mighty men."

"But it is for the praise of God's name I do this, that our tale may be believed, and if I reach Ireland again this piece of silver shall be offered by me on the high altar of Armagh."

And as he cut a piece of the net they heard a voice from the summit of a pillar ringing mighty, clear and distinct. But they knew not the tongue it spoke or the words it uttered.

The next island they stopped at was the Island of the Women. Here they found the rampart of a mighty *dūn* enclosing a mansion. Within the *dūn* they saw eighteen maidens busy at preparing a great bath. In a little while a rider, richly clad, came up swiftly on a racehorse, lighted down, and went inside, with one of the girls taking the horse. The rider then went into the bath which made them realize that she was a woman. Shortly after that one of the maidens came out and invited them to enter.

"The Queen invites you," she said.

They went into the fort and bathed, and then sat down to eat, each man with a maiden over against him, and Maeldūn opposite the Queen. After the meal Maeldūn wedded the Queen and each of the maidens to one of his men. At nightfall canopied chambers were allotted to each of them, and the evening passed pleasantly for all.

On the next morning they made ready to depart, but the Queen would not have them go for she was quite taken with the brave Maeldūn. To persuade them to stay she plied them with sweet promises, saying, "Stay here and old age will never fall on you, but you shall remain as you are now for ever and ever, and what you had last night you shall have always. Do you desire to be wandering from island to island?"

And to Maeldūn she said, "I am the mother of the eighteen girls you have seen and my husband was the king of this island. He is now dead, and I reign in his place. Each day I go into the plain in the interior of the island to judge the folk and at night I return to the *dūn*. Would you not be pleased to join me and help me rule this land as my King?"

Maeldūn, pleased with the offer, decided to remain on the island for a little while longer—or, at the very least, through the three months of winter.

But at the end of that time it seemed they had been there three years, and the men wearied of it, and longed to set forth for their own country.

"What shall we find there," said Maeldūn, "that is better than this?"

But still the men murmured and complained and at last they said, "Great is the love which Maeldūn has for his woman. Let him stay with her alone if he will, but we will go to our own country."

However, Maeldūn realized that he did not want to stay alone on the island without his men so at last one day, when the Queen was away judging the folk, they went on board their bark and put out to sea. Before they had gone far, however, the Queen came riding up with a ball of twine in her hand, and she flung it after them. Maeldūn caught it in his hand, and it clung to his hand so that he could not free himself, and the Queen, holding the other end, drew them back to land. And they stayed on the island for another three months.

Twice again the same thing happened, and at last the

men implied, "Maeldūn holds onto the twine on purpose, so great is his love for the woman."

Maeldūn hotly denied this and said, "If you do not believe that I am drawn back through no free will of my own the next time we set sail another man should catch hold of the twine."

So the next time they prepared to sail out, another man did catch the twine and, it too clung to his hand as it had to Maeldūn's. So Diuran smote it off along with the hand, and both fell into the sea. When the Queen saw this she at once began to wail and shriek, so that all the land was one cry, wailing and shrieking.

Maeldūn, greatly saddened by all his losses, fell into a depression from which no one could arouse him. In the meantime, the ship wandered the ocean for days finding no rest until it came upon the Island of the Eagle. This was a large island with woods of oak and yew on one side of it, and on the other a plain, whereon were herds of sheep, and a little lake. They also found there a small church, a fort, and an ancient gray cleric, clad only in his hair.

"Who are you?" asked Maeldūn.

"I am the fifteenth man of the monks of St. Brennan of Birr," he said. "We went on our pilgrimage into the ocean, and they have all died save me alone." He showed them the calendar of the Holy Brennan, and they prostrated themselves before it, and Maeldūn kissed it.

The monk then said to Maeldūn, "You seem to be in need of some rest and peace from wandering. If you wish you and your men may stay here for a season and feed on the sheep of the island." And Maeldūn, thankful for the offer, accepted.

A few weeks into their stay they saw a great vision. What seemed to be a cloud came up from the southwest and as it drew near, they saw the waving of pinions, and perceived that it was an enormous bird carrying a huge tree-branch as big as a full-grown oak. It came into the island, and alighting very wearily on a hill near the lake, it began eating the red berries which grew like grapes on the tree-branch, and the juice and fragments of the berries fell into the lake, reddening all the water. Fearful that the bird would seize them in its talons and bear them out to sea, the men lay hidden in the woods and watched it.

After a while, however, Maeldūn went out to the foot of the hill, but the bird did him no harm, and then the rest followed cautiously behind their shields. Soon one of them gathered the berries off the branch which the bird held in its talons, but it did them no evil, and regarded them not at all. And they saw that it was very old, its plumage dull and decayed.

At the hour of noon two eagles came up from the southwest and alit in front of the great bird, and after resting awhile they set to work picking off the insects that infested its jaws and eyes and ears. This they continued till vespers, when all three ate of the berries again. At last, on the following day, when the great bird had been completely cleansed, it plunged into the lake, and again the two eagles picked and cleansed it. Until the third day the great bird remained preening and shaking its pinions, and its feathers became glossy and abundant. Then, soaring upwards, it flew thrice around the island, and away to whence it had come, and its flight was now swift and strong.

After seeing the miracle Diuran said, "Let us bathe in

that lake and renew ourselves where the bird has been renewed."

"Nay," said another, "for the bird has left his venom in it." And the others agreed.

So Diuran alone plunged in and drank of the water, and from that time so long as he lived his eyes were strong and keen and not a tooth fell from his jaw nor a hair from his head, and he never knew illness or infirmity.

Thereafter they bade farewell to the anchorite and fared forth on the ocean once more until they arrived at the Island of the Laughing Folk. Here they found a great company of men laughing and playing incessantly, and they started to draw lots as to who should enter and explore it. The last of Maeldūn's foster-brothers, who had remained quiet and withdrawn since the loss of his brothers, volunteered. But as soon as he set foot on the island he at once began to laugh and play with the others, and could not leave off, nor would he come back to his comrades.

So Maeldūn said, "Leave him," and they sailed away.

They drifted again for many days until one morning far off among the waves they saw what they took to be a white bird on the water. Drawing near to it they found it to be an aged man clad only in the white hair of his body, and he was throwing himself in prostrations on a broad rock.

"Who are you and what are you doing?" asked Maeldūn.

"From Torach Island I have come hither," he said, "and there I was reared. I was the cook in the monastery there, and the food of the Church I used to sell for myself, so that I had at last much treasure of raiment and brazen vessels and gold-bound books and all that man desires. Great was my pride and ignorance.

"One day as I dug a grave in which to bury a churl who had been brought on to the island, a voice came from below where a holy man lay buried and said, 'Put not the corpse of a sinner on me, a holy, pious person!'

"After a dispute I buried the corpse elsewhere and was promised an eternal reward for doing so. Not long thereafter I decided to sail away with all my accumulated treasures, meaning to escape from the island with all my plunder. A great wind, however, blew me far out to sea, and when I was out of sight of land the boat stood still in one place.

"I saw near me a man who must have been an angel sitting on the wave. And he told me that I was surrounded by a crowd of demons because of my covetousness and pride, and theft, and other evil deeds. My boat had stopped and it would not move until I promised to do his bidding, and that I immediately promised. He then told me to fling all of my unearned possessions into the sea.

"I thereupon flung everything into the sea save one little wooden cup, and I cast away my oars and rudder. The man gave me a provision of whey and seven cakes, and bade me abide wherever my boat should stop. The wind and waves carried me hither and thither until at last the boat came to rest upon this rock where you have found me. There was nothing here but the bare rock, but remembering what I was bidden I stepped out upon a little ledge over which the waves washed, and the boat immediately left me, and the rock was enlarged for me. Here I have remained seven years, nourished by otters which bring me salmon out of the sea, and even flaming firewood on which to cook them, and my cup is filled with good liquor every day. And neither wet nor heat nor cold affects me in this place."

At the noon hour miraculous nourishment was brought for the whole crew, and thereafter the ancient man said to them, "You will reach your country, and the man that slew your father, O Maeldūn, you will find him in a fortress before you. However, slay him not, but forgive him, because God hath saved you from manifold great perils, and you too are men deserving of death."

They then bade him farewell and went on their now accustomed way. They soon arrived on the Island of the Falcon which was uninhabited save for herds of sheep and oxen. They landed on it and had eaten their fill when one of them saw a large falcon.

"This falcon," he said, "is like the falcons of Ireland."

"Watch it," said Maeldūn, "and see how it will go from us."

The falcon flew off to the southeast and they rowed after it all day until vespers.

At nightfall they sighted a land like Ireland and soon came to a small island, where they ran their prow ashore. It was the island where dwelt the man who had slain Ailill.

They went up to the dūn that was on the island, and heard men talking within it as they sat at dinner.

One man said, "It would be ill for us if we saw Maeldūn now."

"Maeldūn has been drowned," said another.

"Maybe it is he who shall awaken you from sleep tonight," said a third.

"If he should come now," said a fourth, "what should we do?"

"Not hard to answer that," said their chief. "Great welcome should he have if he were to come, for he hath been a long space in great tribulation."

Suddenly the wooden clapper was smote against the door. "Who is there?" asked the doorkeeper.

"Maeldūn is here," said he.

They entered the house in peace and great welcome was made for them and they were arrayed in new garments. Then they told the story of all the marvels that God had shown them and they delighted in the remembrance of these things.

When Maeldūn went to his own home and kindred, his foster-mother greeted him with great delight and celebration—though there was sorrow too in her face after hearing of the loss of her own sons. And the men told many times over the story of all that had befallen them, along with all the marvels they had seen by sea and land, and the perils they had endured.

As for Diuran the Rhymer, he took with him the piece of silver that he had hewn from the net of the pillar and laid it on the high altar of Armagh in triumph and exultation at the miracle that God had wrought for them. ❧